# THE STATE OF ENGLISH IN HIGHER EDUCATION IN TURKEY

A Baseline Study
November 2015

British Council Project Team
Richard West, Consultant
Ayşen Güven, Julian Parry
Tuğçe Ergenekon

TEPAV Project Team
Güneş Aşık, İpek Aydın, Seda Başıhoş, Merve Çankırılı,
Meryem Doğan, Cansu Doğanay, Aycan Kulaksız,
Açelya Gizem Öktem, İdil Özdoğan, Efşan Özen Nas, Berk Yılmaz

British Council

**THE STATE OF ENGLISH
IN HIGHER EDUCATION
IN TURKEY**

A Baseline Study
November 2015

ISBN 978-0-86355-786-6

Publication number:

**Design & Print**
Yorum Basın Yayın Sanayi Ltd. Şti.
İvedik Organize Sanayi Bölgesi Matbaacılar Sitesi
1341. Cadde No: 36 Yenimahalle 06370 ANKARA
Phone: +90 (312) 395 2112
Fax      : +90 (312) 394 1109
www.yorummatbaa.com
info@yorummatbaa.com

**TEPAV**
Türkiye Ekonomi Politikaları Araştırma Vakfı
TOBB-ETÜ Yerleşkesi, TEPAV Binası
Söğütözü Caddesi No: 43 Söğütözü ANKARA
Phone: +90 (312) 292 5500
Fax      : +90 (312) 292 5555
www.tepav.org.tr
tepav@tepav.org.tr

**British Council**
Karum İş Merkezi, İran Caddesi, 21D Blok
Kat 5 No 436 Kavaklıdere-ANKARA, TURKEY
Phone: +90 (312) 455 3600
Fax      : +90 (312) 455 3636

# Foreword

Learning English has been on the agenda of Turkey for many years. Discussions on how to improve the teaching and learning of English is an ongoing issue from the primary to tertiary level.

The British Council supports policy makers, institutions, academics, teachers and learners by providing access to UK expertise in the field of ELT.

In partnership with the Ministry of National Education in Turkey and the Economic Policy Research Foundation (TEPAV), we carried out one of the largest studies of its kind into the teaching of English in state schools in Turkey. Published in November 2013, the study generated great interest from the public and the ELT sector in Turkey and raised issues that are still widely discussed.

With over 175 universities, the majority of which have dedicated English language programmes, the teaching of English in the tertiary sector is a widely discussed issue in Turkey so it was natural for us to seek to extend our understanding of the challenges and successes in English provision in this sector.

The British Council funded and conducted a baseline study into tertiary-level English language provision in the higher education sector in Turkey in 2015. In partnership with TEPAV, we visited 38 universities in 15 cities across Turkey and surveyed leadership teams, academic staff and students. Survey results were supported by class observations.

This report, one of the largest ever carried out into tertiary-level English language teaching in a country, identifies some underlying systemic issues in the Turkish system but also identifies numerous good initiatives in Turkish universities which clearly indicate the commitment to improving the quality of English language teaching at tertiary level. We hope that this report provides valuable contextual data on the areas of strength and the challenges faced by teachers and learners of English at tertiary level.

We would like to express our thanks to all parties involved in the research: the Council of Higher Education for their ongoing support in conducting this study; to all the universities involved in the study; and to TEPAV for their research support.

Julian Parry
Director English and Education Turkey

# Table of contents

Abbreviations and glossary........................................................................................7

Executive summary.................................................................................................13

Preface....................................................................................................................25

Acknowledgements.................................................................................................25

Introduction.............................................................................................................27
Background.............................................................................................................27
Aims and terms of reference...................................................................................30
Structure of report...................................................................................................31
Research methods..................................................................................................31
Research ethics......................................................................................................33

1 International context: globalisation....................................................................35

1.0 The educational revolution...............................................................................35
1.1 University league tables....................................................................................36
1.2 Research..........................................................................................................41
1.3 The Bologna process........................................................................................43
1.4 Quality assurance.............................................................................................44
1.5 Student mobility................................................................................................45
1.6 Staff mobility.....................................................................................................50
1.7 Findings and recommendations.......................................................................51

2 National context: language of instruction..........................................................55

2.0 Introduction......................................................................................................55
2.1 English as medium of instruction (EMI) undergraduate programmes..............56
2.2 Turkish as medium of instruction (TMI) undergraduate programmes..............61
2.3 Mixed medium (T-EMI) undergraduate programmes.......................................63
2.4 Graduate programmes.....................................................................................64
2.5 Findings and recommendations.......................................................................66

3 Institutional context: language teaching programmes.....................................69

3.0 Introduction......................................................................................................69
3.1 Provision and eligibility.....................................................................................69
3.1.1 Language proficiency level............................................................................70
3.1.2 Motivation......................................................................................................71
3.1.3 Compulsion....................................................................................................73
3.2 Distribution of English language programmes.................................................73
3.3 Curriculum........................................................................................................74
3.4 Quality..............................................................................................................76

3.4.1 Assessment and standards..................................................................76
3.4.2 Quality assurance...............................................................................78
3.4.3 Appraisal ............................................................................................78
3.4.4 Continuing Professional Development (CPD)..................................79
3.4.5 Teacher status....................................................................................80
3.5 Findings and recommendations............................................................81

4 Departmental context: English language teaching.................................85

4.0 Introduction............................................................................................85
4.1 Teachers' English proficiency.................................................................85
4.2 Use of mother tongue.............................................................................86
4.3 Teachers' qualifications and training.....................................................86
4.4 Curriculum..............................................................................................87
4.5 Teaching materials..................................................................................88
4.6 Textbook dependence............................................................................89
4.7 Classroom interaction.............................................................................90
4.8 Classroom conditions and resources....................................................91
4.9 Use of technology...................................................................................92
4.10 Findings and recommendations..........................................................93

5 Department context: English as medium of instruction.........................97

5.0 Introduction............................................................................................97
5.1 Approaches to English-mediated education........................................97
5.2 Issues in English-mediated education..................................................99
5.2.1 Introducing EMI..................................................................................99
5.2.2 English language proficiency............................................................100
5.2.3 Responsibility for learning................................................................100
5.2.4 EMI teaching strategies....................................................................101
5.2.5 Training for EMI................................................................................104
5.3 Findings and recommendations..........................................................106

6 Summary findings, recommendations and conclusions.......................109

6.0 Introduction..........................................................................................109
6.1 Findings and recommendations..........................................................109
6.1.1 International context: globalisation..................................................109
6.1.2 National context: language of instruction.......................................110
6.1.3 Institutional context: language teaching programmes..................110
6.1.4 Departmental context: English language teaching.......................111
6.1.5 Departmental context: English as medium of instruction.............112
6.2 Impact analysis: university quality.......................................................112
6.3 Impact analysis: languages of instruction..........................................113
6.4 Impact analysis: English language teaching and learning in universities.........115

6.5 Impact analysis: English as medium of instruction...............................................118
6.6 Conclusions....................................................................................................................119

References..........................................................................................................................121

# Abbreviations and glossary

**ALTE**    **Association of Language Testers of Europe:** An organisation of public language test providers whose examinations are aligned to the Common European Framework of Reference. Turkey is not represented at present.

**BALEAP**    **British Association of Lecturers in English for Academic Purposes:** An organisation of university lecturers teaching academic English to international students. BALEAP has produced schemes for quality assurance and teacher development.

**BRIC**    **Brazil, Russia, India, China:** An abbreviation that identifies four of the main emerging markets of the G20 economies.

**BRICS**    **Brazil, Russia, India, China, South Africa:** An abbreviation that identifies five of the main emerging markets of the G20 economies.

**CEA**    **Commission on English Language Program Accreditation:** A US-based organisation that offers (among other things) a quality assurance scheme for English language programmes. A number of universities in Turkey currently have CEA accreditation.

**CEFR**    **Common European Framework of Reference for Languages:** A Council of Europe document published in 2001 that sets out standards for foreign-language teaching at six levels (A1, A2, B1, B2, C1, C2). Turkey is a member of the Council of Europe and the levels of the CEFR should therefore be adopted for all foreign-language courses in Turkish universities. Most students currently enter university preparatory schools with a CEFR level of A1+ and are expected to reach B2 in a period of eight months.

| C2 | Advanced |
|----|----------|
| C1 |          |
| B2 | ↑        |
| B1 |          |
| A2 |          |
| A1 | Elementry |

**CELTA**    **Certificate in Teaching English to Speakers of Other Languages:** An initial qualification for teachers of English to Speakers of Other Languages provided by Cambridge Assessment, UK. CELTA is offered in some centres in Turkey.

**CFL**    **Centre for Foreign Languages:** A university department in which foreign languages are taught to undergraduates and, sometimes, graduate students and staff.

**CLIL**    **Content and Language Integrated Learning:** An approach to academic teaching (e.g. the teaching of Economics, Science, Medicine,) in which the academic faculty member or teacher takes some responsibility for the language used to deliver the content and tries to accommodate the language problems of his/her students. (Compare **EMI**.)

**CoE**    **Council of Europe:** A political, cultural, educational and legal association of European nations. Turkey is a member.

**CoHE**    **The Council of Higher Education (Yükseköğretim Kurulu):** The body responsible for overseeing higher education in Turkey (usually abbreviated as YÖK).

**DEDAK**    **Dil Eğitimi Değerlendirme ve Akreditasyon Kurulu (Language Training Evaluation and Accreditation Council):** An association committed to quality assurance and standards in language courses in Turkish universities.

**DELTA**    **Diploma in Teaching English to Speakers of Other Languages:** An advanced qualification for teachers of English to speakers of other languages provided by Cambridge Assessment, UK. DELTA is offered in some centres in Turkey.

**DS**    **Diploma Supplement:** A document offered to international students describing the courses and/or qualifications they have taken while studying overseas. The DS is a Bologna requirement and is offered by most Turkish universities.

**EAP**    **English for Academic Purposes:** The kind of English required for university study, e.g. reading academic books or journals, writing academic assignments or papers, listening to academic lectures, and taking part in academic discussion. EAP is usually divided into general (EGAP) and specific (ESAP).

**EAQUALS**    **Evaluation and Accreditation of Quality in Language Services:** A European quality assurance scheme for adult language programmes. One university in Turkey currently has EAQUALS accreditation.

**ECTS**    **European Credit Transfer System:** A system that describes the objectives, learning outcomes and study budget of any university course or programme. ECTS is a Bologna requirement.

**EF**    **Education First:** A Swiss-based educational organisation (formerly known as English First) that provides language courses and also produces the annual English Proficiency Index (EPI).

**EfA**    **English for Academics:** A type of EAP intended for academics, university lecturers and researchers.

**EFL**    **English as a Foreign Language:** The situation in countries (e.g. Turkey) where English is not the mother tongue of the majority of the population and has no formal administrative role.

**EGAP**    **English for General Academic Purposes:** A branch of English language teaching (ELT). The type of Academic English (EAP) that is taught to all students, regardless of their academic discipline or major. Usually contrasted with English for Specific Academic Purposes (ESAP).

**EGOP**    **English for General Occupational Purposes:** A branch of English language teaching (ELT) concerned with the type of occupational English (EOP) that is taught to all trainees, regardless of their profession or job. Usually contrasted with ESOP. (See Figure 1.)

**EGP**    **English for General Purposes:** A branch of English language teaching (ELT). The type of English that is usually taught in schools and which is not related to a particular study or occupational purpose. Usually contrasted with ESP. (See Figure 1.)

**ELFA**    **English as a Lingua Franca in Academic Settings:** The type of English used by non-native academics.

**ELT**   **English language teaching:** The profession of teaching English to speakers of other languages. ELT includes several main branches:

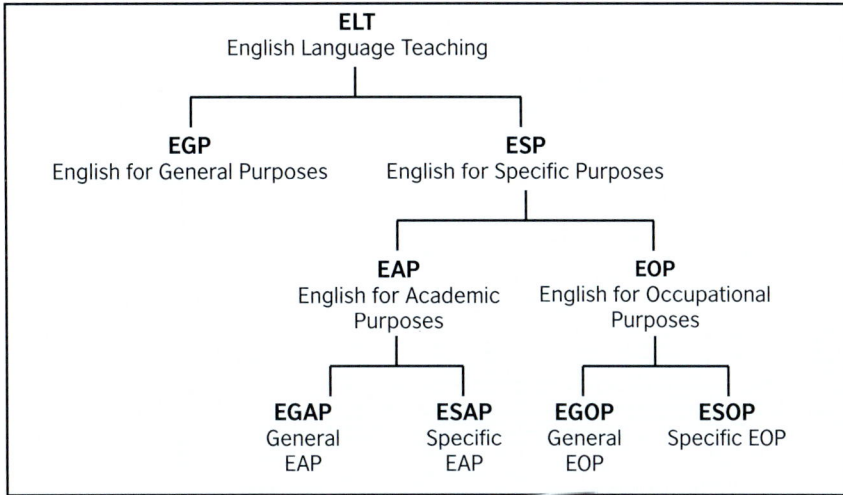

Figure 1: Branches of English language teaching (based on Jordan 1998)

**EME**   **English-Medium Education/English-Mediated Education:** Education which is delivered through the medium of the English language.

**EMI**   **English as a/the Medium of Instruction:** Teaching which is delivered through the medium of the English language. (See **CLIL**.)

**EOP**   **English for Occupational Purposes:** A branch of English language teaching (ELT) that is concerned with teaching the kind of English that relates to a person's occupation or job, e.g. writing business letters, making business phone calls, reading professional reports, giving a business presentation, etc. (See Figure 1.)

**EPI**   **English Proficiency Index:** An online English test administered by Education First (EF) which is used to draw up an annual index or ranking of countries' English proficiency. Turkey took part of the latest 2014 EPI of 63 countries and achieved 47th rank.

**ESAP**   **English for Specific Academic Purposes:** A branch of English language teaching (ELT) concerned with teaching the academic language of a particular discipline (e.g. Economics, Psychology, etc). This includes specialist terminology and the conventions for writing particular documents. Usually contrasted with EGAP. (See Figure 1.)

**ESOP**   **English for Specific Occupational Purposes:** A branch of English language teaching (ELT) concerned with teaching the occupational language of a particular profession (e.g. accountants, airline pilots, doctors, etc). This includes specialist terminology and the conventions for writing

| | |
|---|---|
| | particular documents. Usually contrasted with EGOP. (See Figure 1.) |
| ESP | **English for Specific Purposes:** A branch of English language teaching (ELT) concerned with teaching the language needed for a particular purpose. Usually divided into English for Academic Purposes (EAP) and English for Occupational Purposes (EOP). (See Figure 1.) |
| EU | **European Union:** The economic and political association of European countries. |
| HE | **Higher education:** The sector of education, including universities, which delivers degree-level programmes and conducts research. |
| HEI | **Higher education institution:** A university or an institution that delivers degree-level programmes and conducts research. |
| IELTS | **International English Language Testing System**: A UK-based English examination used to assess language proficiency according to a system of nine 'bands'. Widely used for university entrance and occupational purposes. |
| IWB | **Interactive whiteboard:** A large interactive display that connects to a computer. A projector projects the computer's desktop images onto the board's surface where users control the computer using a pen, finger, stylus, or other device. The board is typically mounted to a wall or floor stand. |
| L1 | **First language:** A person's native language or mother tongue (MT). |
| L2 | **Second language:** A language that is acquired or learned after childhood. Usually contrasted with their first language (L1). |
| MI | **Medium of Instruction:** The language used for teaching. In this study there are three main MIs – Turkish (TMI), English (EMI) and mixed Turkish-English medium (T-EMI). |
| MIST | **Mexico, Indonesia, South Korea, Turkey:** An economic term referring to four of the emerging economies of the G20 countries. |
| MT | **Mother tongue:** A person's first language (L1) or mother tongue (MT). |
| N | **Number:** The total number of participants or cases in an experiment or survey. |
| NNS | **Non-native speaker:** Someone who does not speak a language as their mother tongue (MT). |
| NS | **Native speaker:** Someone who speaks a language as their mother tongue (MT). |
| PhD | **Doctor of Philosophy:** The third or top tier of higher education under the Bologna system. |
| QA | **Quality assurance:** A system that provides a full and regular check on the quality of an educational institution. A requirement of the Bologna process. |
| QS | **Quacquarelli Symonds:** A UK-based organisation that compiles annual rankings of the world's top universities. |
| RAE | **Research assessment exercise:** A regular system for assessing the quality of university research. |
| SETA | **Siyaset, Ekonomi ve Toplum Araştırmaları Vakfı (Foundation for Political, Economic and Social Research):** A non-profit research institute |

| | dedicated to innovative studies on national, regional, and international issues. |
|---|---|
| TA | **Teaching assistant:** Someone, typically a PhD student, employed by a university to help teach undergraduates. |
| T-EMI | **Turkish and English as Languages of Instruction:** Mixed-medium teaching delivered through a mixture of Turkish and English. |
| TEPAV | **Türkiye Ekonomi Politikaları Araştırma Vakfı (Economic Policy Research Foundation of Turkey):** A non-partisan, non-profit think tank based in Ankara, Turkey. TEPAV is the research partner of this study. |
| THES | **Times Higher Educational Supplement:** A UK-based weekly newspaper specialising in university education. One of its publications is an annual ranking of the world's top universities. |
| TL | **Target language:** The language that a person is trying to learn on a language course. |
| TMI | **Turkish as a Medium of Instruction:** Teaching which is delivered through the medium of the Turkish language. |
| TNNA | **Turkey National Needs Assessment:** Turkey National Needs Assessment of State School English Language Teaching Report published by the British Council and TEPAV in 2013. (Vale *et al* 2013). |
| TOEFL | **Test of English as a foreign language:** A US-based examination of general English as a foreign language which is widely used for university entrance purposes. |
| URAP | **University Ranking by Academic Performance:** An annual university ranking system compiled by Middle East Technical University, Ankara. |
| USSR | **Union of Soviet Socialist Republics:** The former Soviet Union. |
| YÖDEK | **Yükseköğretim Kurumları Akademik Değerlendirme ve Kalite Geliştirme Komisyonu (Commission for Academic Assessment and Quality Improvement in Higher Education):** A Turkish organisation for assessment in higher education. |
| YÖK | **Yükseköğretim Kurulu (The Council of Higher Education):** The body responsible for overseeing higher education in Turkey (usually abbreviated in English as CoHE). |

# Executive summary

In November 2013 the British Council and TEPAV carried out large-scale research into the teaching of English in state schools in Turkey[1]. The Turkey National Needs Assessment (TNNA) report examined the economic importance of English to Turkey and carried out detailed research into the classroom teaching of English. It concluded that Turkey is underperforming in the area of English language teaching (ELT) and that this 'deficit' is the result of inadequate teaching in primary and secondary schools. Furthermore, this English deficiency could threaten Turkey's economic development. The report went on to identify five key limitations in ELT in Turkey and to make five key recommendations to address them.

Following the publication of the TNNA, it was proposed that there should be a similar study of ELT in Turkish universities. The British Council undertook to fund and conduct this survey, which is described as a 'baseline study'. The approach of the baseline study is to look for examples of good practice in one university which could be disseminated elsewhere, so that the system could be reformed by applying what can be learned from best practice elsewhere. The findings and recommendations reflect this approach – nearly all the recommendations are based on examples and innovations already in operation in universities in Turkey.

The aim of the baseline study was specified through two broad questions:

> "What are the conditions in which pre- and in-sessional courses of English are offered in public and foundation universities in Turkey and how can these conditions be enhanced?"

A broad interpretation of the basic research questions led the researchers to examine English teaching at five interrelated contextual levels:

1  International context: globalisation

2  National context: medium of instruction

3  Institutional context: language teaching

4  Departmental context: English language teaching

5  Departmental context: English as medium of instruction

Each of these levels is explored fully in the chapters of the report, based on lesson observations, questionnaires, structured interviews and focus groups carried out over a five-week period in March–April 2015. Each chapter concludes with a summary of the major findings, which are then matched with conclusions in the final chapter. The key findings and summary recommendations are set out below:

---

[1] *Vale et al* 2013

1. **International context: globalisation**

| **Findings:** In contrast to other G20 countries, Turkey has focused on quantity in recent years by significantly expanding the number and size of its universities. While there has also been an improvement in quality, with a number of universities performing well in the *Times Higher Education Supplement* global university rankings, there are 100 Turkish universities that fall outside the world's top 2,000 universities according to Turkey's own URAP rankings. Turkey's 'English deficit' is a major factor affecting the quality of higher education, restricting access to academic resources, international research publication and the mobility of staff and students. | **Recommendation:** *Consideration should be given to creating and funding a project to enhance the quality of universities in Turkey. This would have two major aims:* <br> **a)** *To identify and support a tier of high-quality research universities in the top 200 in the global league tables.* <br> **b)** *To enhance the quality of teaching, research and resources in the large number of universities that currently fall outside the top 1,000 in the URAP rankings.* <br> *English proficiency levels of students and, in particular, academic staff should form a key part of this project.* |
|---|---|

**Recommendations:** See Section 1.7.

2. **National context: medium of instruction**

| **Findings:** Turkey has a long history of university education in both Turkish medium (TMI) and English medium (EMI), and, more recently, mixed-medium Turkish-English instruction (T-EMI). While EMI universities have traditionally been 'more favoured and popular for students and parents in comparison to universities without EMI'[2], there are strong arguments for strengthening the quantity and quality of TMI programmes, in particular because the current English proficiency levels of both academic staff and students restrict effective learning. Mixed-medium T-EMI teaching has, from the evidence in this survey, proved largely ineffective, with staff and | **Recommendation:** *It is recommended that more focus, status and resources should be given to TMI programmes. While it is not recommended that EMI programmes should be phased out, it is suggested that parallel TMI programmes should be introduced (as already happens in some universities in Turkey) and students should be permitted to access programmes and be assessed in either or both languages. No new mixed-medium T-EMI programmes should be authorised and existing T-EMI programmes should be phased out as soon as possible. It is calculated that this parallel TMI-EMI model would be* |
|---|---|

[2] Başıbek *et al* 2013: 1819

| | |
|---|---|
| students developing strategies for circumventing the use of English in favour of Turkish. | more cost effective than the current mixed-medium programmes. |

**Recommendations:** See Section 2.5.

3. Institutional context: language teaching

| | |
|---|---|
| **Findings:** The current distribution and curriculum of English language teaching in Turkish universities do not give full support to the academic programmes or internationalisation. Students enter preparatory school with low English proficiency levels and low motivation. Preparatory school classes do not fully address these problems as the curriculum is perceived to be lacking in relevance and the classes are not delivered at the time in a student's academic career when they could be most effective. | *Recommendation: Systemic changes should be made in three areas:*<br>***a) Eligibility and standards:*** *Preparatory classes should be voluntary and normally available only to EMI students. The threshold for both entry to and exit from preparatory school should be raised and assessed through valid examinations assessing all four skills in order to ensure that standards are met and maintained. Students who do not meet these standards should be redirected to TMI programmes or universities.*<br>***b) Curriculum:*** *The curriculum should be shifted away from English for General Purposes (EGP) towards English for General Academic Purposes (EGAP), and EGAP classes should be customised to cater for students' specialist academic fields. An elective English for Occupational Purposes (EOP) course should be available in the final undergraduate year for those seeking jobs. The curriculum for all of these programmes should be based on a full needs analysis.*<br>***c) Distribution:*** *Credit-bearing English language courses should be maintained throughout all undergraduate and graduate programmes. These courses should be requirements for all EMI students but elective for TMI students.* |

**Recommendations:** See Section 3.5.

4. **Departmental context: English language teaching**

| Findings: The English proficiency levels and qualifications of English teachers in universities are very good, but two widespread shortcomings were observed:<br>**a)** Most teachers have little or no training in the teaching of EAP/ESP and consequently they lack the skills to develop needs-based EGAP curricula or to customise materials and activities to fit the specialist academic disciplines of students.<br>**b)** Most teachers constantly miss opportunities to introduce student-student interaction in the classroom. In the short term, this reduces students' progress in speaking skills; in the longer-term it undermines their confidence and ability to participate in class discussion or debate on their academic undergraduate programmes. | **Recommendation:** English teachers should have greater opportunities to access professional development as part of a quality assurance and accreditation scheme. In particular, training should be available in two key areas:<br>**EAP/ESP:** All English teachers should undergo a short, intensive training programme in EAP/ESP[3], and some teachers in each university should be offered longer-term training such as that available by distance from some universities.[4]<br>**Teaching speaking skills:** All teachers should undergo training in techniques for incorporating student-student interaction at every stage of the lesson, with speaking integrated into every activity, regardless of the skill being practised. ELT publishers may offer such training as part of the package of materials sold to a university. |
|---|---|

**Recommendations:** See Section 4.10.

5. **Departmental context: English as medium of instruction**

| Findings: The English proficiency levels of EMI academics generally meet international standards, but there are problems in some universities in finding enough academics with adequate levels of English to meet current requirements or expand EMI programmes. EMI academics do not generally accommodate students' language difficulties and regard EMI learning | **Recommendation:** The approach to English-mediated education should be shifted from EMI to CLIL (Content and Language Integrated Learning) in line with developments in most European countries. EMI academics should be required to undergo training to take more responsibility for their students' learning by adopting a range of language and technological strategies to facilitate learning. |
|---|---|

---
[3] Perhaps based on Day and Krzanowski 2011
[4] e.g. the distance MA modules in EAP/ESP offered by the universities such as the University of Reading or the University of Nottingham in the UK

| | |
|---|---|
| as the students' responsibility. This approach arises because few academics have been offered any training in EMI teaching and little training of this kind seems to be available in Turkish universities. | |

**Recommendations:** See Section 5.3.

In the following sections, the recommendations are set out in slightly more detail, and the likely impact of each recommendation is analysed.

**Impact analysis: university quality**

While other emerging G20 countries such as Russia, China, India and South Korea have launched projects to enhance the quality and standing of their universities, Turkey has focused on quantity and instituted a massive expansion of university student numbers. It is recommended that the Turkish government should launch a similar project to improve the quality of universities. In this section a summary is given of what could be achieved if the recommendations of this report are implemented in full:

| Step | Action | Recommendation | Impact |
|---|---|---|---|
| 1 | **Support for research universities** | *Create and fund a project to identify and support a tier of high-quality research universities in the top 200 in the global league tables.* | This would enable top Turkish universities to maintain and improve their rankings. The project would involve many initiatives (enhanced resources, improved qualifications, travel opportunities, quality assurance, research assessment etc.), but it would also require improving the English-language proficiency of academic staff. Improved English would facilitate:<br>• international research collaboration |

| Step | Action | Recommendation | Impact |
|---|---|---|---|
|  |  |  | • research publication and dissemination<br>• the development of new postgraduate programmes<br>• attracting more international students from outside the Turkic-/Turkish-speaking region<br>• attracting international staff. |
| 2 | **Support for research inactive universities** | *Create and fund a project to enhance the quality of teaching, research and resources in the large number of universities that currently fall outside the top 1,000 in the URAP rankings.* | The project would aim to enhance the academic quality and research capability of these universities. This would also require improved English proficiency of academic staff, which would facilitate:<br>• access to academic resources in English to inform Turkish-medium teaching and research<br>• promotion in the URAP rankings for these universities. |

**Impact analysis: languages of instruction**
The languages used for instruction in Turkish universities vary and often undermine academic needs and efficiency. The entry level of most students is too low to benefit fully from EMI tuition, even after a year of preparatory school. Students mostly want English for longer-term occupational reasons rather than academic needs. In this report three recommendations are made regarding the languages used for

instruction. In this section a summary is given of what could be achieved if the recommendations of this report are implemented in full:

| Step | Action | Recommendation | Impact |
|---|---|---|---|
| 1 | Turkish-medium instruction | *It is recommended that more focus, status and resources should be given to TMI programmes.* | Turkish-medium programmes would become more attractive to students and parents. Students would learn their specialist subjects more efficiently in their mother tongue, improving academic quality. |
| | | *It is suggested that TMI programmes should be introduced parallel to existing EMI programmes, and that students should be permitted to access programmes in either or both languages, and should able to choose which language they are assessed in.* | Students wanting an element of EMI would be able to access lectures in English. International students could access EMI programmes. Academic staff would gain practice in teaching in English. |
| 2 | English-medium instruction | *While it is not recommended that current undergraduate EMI programmes should be phased out, it is suggested that new ones should not be introduced until secondary schools produce graduates with CEFR B1 levels of English proficiency.* | The academic quality of programmes would not be threatened by students' inadequate levels of English proficiency. |
| | | *It is also recommended that the focus of new EMI programmes should be at the graduate rather than the undergraduate level.* | More graduate EMI programmes would attract more international students and staff. |

| Step | Action | Recommendation | Impact |
|---|---|---|---|
| 3 | **Mixed-medium instruction** | *No new mixed-medium T-EMI programmes should be authorised, and existing ones phased out as soon as possible, and replaced by parallel EMI and TMI programmes.* | Students could concentrate on their academic subjects without having their progress impeded by trying to comprehend content delivered in English. Academic quality and motivation would be improved. |

**Impact analysis: English language teaching and learning in universities**

In this report, the current situation in Turkish universities has been surveyed at a number of levels: international, national, institutional and departmental. It is evident that the root cause of Turkey's 'English deficit' is the problems in the school system and that these will take a generation to rectify. In the meantime, universities have little choice but to operate with an intake whose English level is 'rudimentary; even after 1,000+ hours (estimated at end of Grade 12) of English classes'.[5] Under these circumstances (as is stated in Section 3.1.1) it is 'virtually impossible'[6] to reach the target level of B2 in the eight months of the preparatory school programme – they are expected to do too much with too many students in too little time. The central problem is students' motivation, and all the measures set out here are aimed at improving motivation.

In this section a summary is given of what could be achieved if certain recommendations of this report are implemented in full in a series of 11 steps:

| Step | Action | Recommendation | Impact |
|---|---|---|---|
| 1 | **Reduced eligibility** | *Preparatory classes should normally be available only to EMI students.* | Reduced intake and improved motivation as English classes are seen as broadly relevant to the medium of instruction. |
| 2 | **Raised entry standard** | *The threshold for entry for EMI students should be raised to CEFR A2.* | Improved intake, although it must be stated that by European standards CEFR A2 is still very low. |

[5] Vale *et al* 2013:16
[6] Vale *et al* 2013:16

| Step | Action | Recommendation | Impact |
|---|---|---|---|
| 3 | Improved entry assessment | The entry level should be assessed through valid university entrance examinations assessing all four skills. | The university entrance examinations will provide a motivating target for candidates. |
| 4 | Revised curriculum | The curriculum should be shifted away from English for General Purposes (EGP) towards English for General Academic Purposes (EGAP), and EGAP classes should be customised to cater for students' specialist academic fields. | Motivation will be improved because students would not be repeating what they failed to learn several times in school, and because they will now see the relevance of the curriculum to their academic studies. |
| 5 | In-service teacher development | All English teachers should undergo a short, intensive training programme in EAP/ EAP, and some teachers in each university should be offered longer-term training such as that available by distance from some universities. | English teachers will have the confidence and the skills to teach a more relevant curriculum, using materials which they could adapt and customise to students' academic disciplines. Students' extrinsic motivation would be improved by a curriculum and materials which are perceived as relevant. |
| 6 | Communicative methodology | All teachers should undergo training in techniques for incorporating student-student interaction at every stage of the lesson, with speaking integrated into every activity, regardless of the skill being practised. | Teachers would have the skills and confidence to deliver more interactive lessons. Students' speaking skills and confidence would be improved. Students' intrinsic motivation would be improved by more dynamic lessons. |
| 7 | Revised exit standards | The exit standards for preparatory school should be revised: | If stages 1-6 are implemented, these exit standards are |

| Step | Action | Recommendation | Impact |
|---|---|---|---|
| | | CEFR B2 in all skills for linguistically-demanding programmes[7] ; CEFR B1+ in all skills for linguistically less-demanding programmes[8] . | a) achievable and b) minimally adequate for EMI study. They would provide realistic and motivating standards for students. |
| 8 | Improved exit assessment | The exit level should be assessed through valid preparatory school exit examinations assessing all four skills. | A rigorous and valid exit examination would provide a realistic and motivating standard for students and a positive 'washback effect'. |
| 9 | Redirection | Students who do not meet these exit standards should be redirected to TMI programmes or universities. | Another stage providing extrinsic motivation. Note: It is also recommended that the status and resources of TMI programmes should be improved so that they are not seen as 'second best'. |
| 10 | Revised distribution of English teaching programmes | Credit-bearing English language courses should be maintained throughout all undergraduate and graduate programmes. These courses should be requirements for all EMI students but elective for TMI students. | Students would receive the English language support they need throughout all the years of their undergraduate and (where appropriate) graduate study. |
| 11 | Work-related English | An elective English for Occupational Purposes (EOP) course should be available in the final undergraduate year for those seeking jobs. | All students would have an opportunity to acquire work-related English at a time when they will be most motivated to learn it. |

## Impact analysis: English as medium of instruction

Although the English proficiency of most academics teaching through English is adequate, two major problems have been identified:

---
[7] e.g. Engineering, Pure Sciences, Medicine, Law, Journalism, Business, etc
[8] e.g. Technology, Pure Mathematics, Agriculture, etc

- Senior academics in many institutions reported that there is a shortage of academics with the necessary levels of English proficiency to teach their specialist subjects.
- The teaching styles of most EMI academics fail to accommodate the language problems of their students.

| Step | Action | Recommendation | Impact |
|---|---|---|---|
| 1 | **Improved EMI teaching** | *The approach to English-mediated education should be shifted from traditional English Medium Instruction (EMI), where the lecturer takes little or no responsibility for the language used, to Content and Language Integrated Learning (CLIL), in which the lecturer uses strategies that take account of students' language limitations, in line with developments in most European countries.* | Academic lecturers would feel more confident and effective when teaching through the medium of English.<br><br>Students would receive the English language support they need throughout their undergraduate and (where appropriate) graduate study. |
| 2 | **Training for EMI lecturers** | *EMI academics should be required to undergo training and to take responsibility for their students' learning by adopting a range of language and technological strategies to facilitate learning.* | Students' learning load would be reduced as lecturers 'accommodate' their language limitations and employ strategies to ensure that communication and motivation are improved in the academic classroom. |

# Preface

## Project members and roles

**The British Council**, the United Kingdom's international organisation for cultural relations and educational opportunities, is registered as a charity in the United Kingdom and has offices in 110 countries, including Turkey. The British Council has built up substantial experience and expertise in the field of educational reform, with particular reference to the teaching and learning of English. In Turkey, the British Council is able to call on in-house expertise as well as access to a network of UK experience and international consultants. The British Council funded the current project and was responsible for its overall management, under the direction of the Project Manager.

**Richard West** was the British Council's consultant for this project. After teaching for 20 years at the University of Manchester, in 2005 he formed ABC Language Consultants, which specialises in the evaluation of projects, institutions and national baseline studies in English language teaching. Recent consultancies have included project and institutional evaluations in Egypt, Uzbekistan, Russia and Saudi Arabia, and baseline studies in Russia and Ukraine. On this project, Richard West drew up the research instruments, conducted the lesson observations, teachers' interviews and departmental profiles, and drafted the final report.

**TEPAV** The Economic Policy Research Foundation of Turkey (TEPAV) is a non-partisan, non-profit think tank based in Ankara, Turkey. It was founded in 2004 by a group of business people, bureaucrats and academics who believe in the power of knowledge and ideas in shaping Turkey's future. Aiming to contribute to public policy design, TEPAV seeks to enrich the knowledge content in Turkey's discussions. TEPAV carries out projects which actively contribute to economic development and bring together key policy and opinion makers to tackle the problems of the day, and has great experience of survey design and large-scale research. On this project, TEPAV was responsible for putting together the fieldwork programme, contributing to the design of the research instruments, distributing and analysing the research questionnaires and institutional profiles.

## Acknowledgements

The British Council would like to thank the Council of Higher Education (CoHE) for supporting the research throughout the planning and fieldwork stages.

The British Council would also like to thank all the institutions, officials and teachers that took part in the research for their assistance in arranging programmes and setting up meetings, focus groups and observations, for their co-operation in distributing and completing questionnaires, and for their hospitality throughout the fieldwork.

# Introduction

## Background

In November 2013 the British Council and TEPAV carried out large-scale research into the teaching of English in state schools in Turkey (Vale *et al*, 2013). The Turkey National Needs Assessment (TNNA) report examined the economic importance of English to Turkey and carried out detailed research into the classroom teaching of English. It concluded that Turkey is underperforming in the area of English language teaching and that this deficiency could threaten Turkey's economic development:

> **Turkey is yet to catch up with competitor economies in its level of English language proficiency.** Turkey consistently ranks very low on various measures of English language speaking. For example, the 2013 English Proficiency Index (EPI) developed by English First puts Turkey 41st out of 60 countries. In 2012, the average total Test of English as a Foreign Language (TOEFL) score of both native Turkish speakers and residents of Turkey was 75 over 120, similar to countries which do not have a Latin alphabet, such as Sudan and Ethiopia.

Turkey's position has not improved since 2012. In the 2014 English Proficiency Index, Turkey came 47th in the world and last of the 24 European countries:

| European Ranking | World Ranking | Country | European Ranking | World Ranking | Country |
|---|---|---|---|---|---|
| 1 | 1 | Denmark | 13 | 16 | Romania |
| 2 | 2 | Netherlands | 14 | 17 | Hungary |
| 3 | 3 | Sweden | 15 | 18 | Switzerland |
| 4 | 4 | Finland | 16 | 19 | Czech Republic |
| 5 | 5 | Norway | 17 | 20 | Spain |
| 6 | 6 | Poland | 18 | 21 | Portugal |
| 7 | 7 | Austria | 19 | 22 | Slovakia |
| 8 | 8 | Estonia | 20 | 27 | Italy |
| 9 | 9 | Belgium | 21 | 29 | France |
| 10 | 10 | Germany | 22 | 36 | Russia |
| 11 | 11 | Slovenia | 23 | 44 | Ukraine |
| 12 | 14 | Latvia | 24 | 47 | Turkey |

Figure 2: European rankings of English proficiency 2014 (EPI 2014)

From Figure 2 it can be seen that there is a close relationship between English proficiency and economic standing.[9] Turkey comes bottom of the table with the poorest EPI performance in Europe and is out-performed by several countries (e.g.

---

[9] EF reports positive correlations between national EPI scores and such indicators as exports per capita, gross national income per capita, service exports, and quality of life. Writing in the Harvard Business Review blog, EF Senior Vice President Christopher McCormick adds:
"Research shows a direct correlation between the English skills of a population and the economic performance of the country. Indicators like gross national income (GNI) and GDP go up... [The 2013 EPI] found that in almost every one of the 60 countries and territories surveyed, a rise in English proficiency was connected with a rise in per capita income. And on an individual level, recruiters and HR managers around the world report that job seekers with exceptional English compared to their country's level earned 30–50 % higher salaries."(ICEF Monitor 29 January 2014)

Romania, Ukraine[10]) with weaker economic indicators.

Having established that Turkey has an 'English deficit', the 2013 report goes on to examine the reasons, and focuses on poor standards of teaching in state schools at primary and secondary levels:

> This study, which identifies the reasons behind the relatively low level of success in English language teaching and learning in the state educational system, identified two major realities:
>
> **A** Teachers: Most (80+% teachers have the qualifications and language skills to deliver effective language lessons so the majority of the student population of Turkey will graduate from High School in Grade 12 with at least an intermediate level of speaking, listening, reading and writing competences in English.
>
> **B** Students: Despite the potential of the teachers and a positive classroom environment, the competence level in English of most (90+% students across Turkey was evidenced as rudimentary – even after 1,000+ hours (estimated at the end of Grade 12) of English classes.[11]

This failure of schools to teach English at anything beyond 'rudimentary' levels is the central 'reality' identified by the Turkey National Needs Assessment (TNNA). It is also the major factor underlying the problems of English language teaching at university level.

This report, which was published in 2013 by the British Council and TEPAV, also identified five major factors which underlie these realities and made recommendations which are intended to address the problems and enhance English language learning across the country.

| Findings | Recommendation |
|---|---|
| More than 80 per cent of observed teachers have the professional competence and language level to meet requirements as teachers of English. However, the teaching of English as a subject and not a language of communication was observed in all schools visited. | Develop a comprehensive and sustainable system of in-service teacher training for English teachers.[12] |
| In all classes observed, students fail to learn how to communicate and function independently in English. | This should aim to raise competences with regard to contemporary English language teaching methodologies and outcomes. In particular, these should focus on teaching English as a tool of communication, (as opposed to teaching 'grammar'). |

---

[10] The per capita income of Turkey is US$10,815; that of Romania is US$8,635 and Ukraine US$2,542 (Source: International Monetary Fund).
[11] Vale et al 2013: 15-16; it will be noted that initial teacher training and school-leaving/university entrance examinations were not mentioned as factors contributing to the 'English deficit'.
[12] This recommendation of the TNNA is echoed in the present report; see Chapter 6.

| Findings | Recommendation |
|---|---|
| Almost all classrooms observed had a layout where students sit together, in pairs on bench seats. However, teachers fail to use this seating arrangement to organise students into pairs and groups for independent, communicative language practice in everyday classroom contexts. | Integrate and manage pair and group work in everyday classroom practice; |
| At present, official textbooks and curricula fail to take account of the varying levels and needs of students. | Develop a revised curriculum document, and related learning materials, including text-books. The above-mentioned, revised curriculum document and learning materials, should demonstrate realistic progression from Grade 2 to Grade 12. |
| Teachers interviewed stated they have little voice in the process and practice of teaching English. Interviews with stakeholders and teachers indicated that the present Inspectorate are non-specialists in English language teaching, are usually non-English speakers, and do not/are unable to provide advice or support to teachers during school visits. | Over a 5-10 year period, the role of English-teaching inspections should transform to that of inspection plus supervision. For English, inspectors should be specialists in the subject. It is therefore recommended that the Ministry should consider recruiting for this revised role from the classroom, where senior teachers or those recognised for their abilities in the teaching of English may apply.[13] |

Following the publication of TNNA, it was proposed that a similar study for higher education would be valuable. The British Council undertook to fund and conduct this survey, which is described as a 'baseline study'. A baseline study may be defined as research carried out to identify in detail the current situation in an education system, sector or institution. In particular, a baseline study usually has the following features:

- it identifies areas where reform or change may be needed
- it makes recommendations about how these reforms might be implemented
- it provides a base against which change can be compared after the reforms have been introduced.

This baseline study, one of the largest ever carried out into university English language teaching in a country, seeks for examples of good practice in one university

---

[13] Five factors that account for poor levels of English in high schools (Vale *et al* 2013:16-17, 54, 56)

which could be disseminated elsewhere, so that the system could be reformed by applying what can be learned from best practice elsewhere. The findings and recommendations reflect this approach: nearly all the recommendations are based on examples and innovations already in operation in universities in Turkey.

## Aims and terms of reference

The aim of the baseline study was specified through two broad questions:

> "What are the conditions in which pre- and in-sessional courses of English are offered in public and foundation universities in Turkey?" and "How can these conditions be enhanced?"

These questions involve both *description* of the present conditions and *recommendations* about how these conditions could be enhanced. The term 'conditions' is taken to mean not only the physical and organisational conditions under which English is taught in Turkish universities, but also the conditions imposed by various international, national and institutional bodies on teachers of English. Furthermore, the phrase 'courses of English' has been taken to include not only straightforward English language lessons of the type that are concentrated in preparatory courses, but also programmes taught through the medium of English at undergraduate and graduate levels.

This broad interpretation of the basic research questions has led the researchers to examine English teaching at four interrelated contextual levels, each of which may be of particular interest and relevance to different audiences:

**International context: globalisation**
(Bologna Process, university internationalisation, etc)

▼

**National context: medium of instruction**

▼

**Institutional context: language teaching**

▼                                                                 ▼

**Departmental context**

a) English language teaching             b) English as medium of instruction

## Structure of report
Each of these contexts will be explored in the following chapters. The structure of the report follows this contextual framework within which English is taught in Turkish universities:

1. International context: globalisation

2. National context: medium of instruction

3. Institutional context: language teaching

4. Departmental context: English language teaching

5. Departmental context: English as medium of instruction

This structure also reflects a major departure from the approach of the needs assessment of English teaching in schools – while the 2013 report necessarily focused on the institutional and departmental contexts of English language teaching[14], the present research is much broader, exploring the wider international issues that affect ELT in Turkish universities.

## Research methods
This baseline study involved large-scale research carried out in March–April 2015 in 38 universities, selected in agreement with CoHE, to include a broad mix of:

- English-medium, Turkish-medium and mixed-medium universities
- state universities and foundation universities
- old universities and new universities
- large universities and small universities.

To ensure a geographical spread and representativeness, the study was conducted in 15 cities in different regions across Turkey. The research employed a range of quantitative and qualitative methods. Wherever possible, the findings are supported by at least two sources of data in order to ensure validity. The different research methods included the following:

- **Questionnaires**
  Questionnaires were constructed for English teachers, students and academics using English as their medium of instruction. These questionnaires were constructed to parallel each other so that results from one group of stakeholders could be readily compared with those from another. The questionnaires were piloted, and then reviewed by the three project partners. They were distributed during five weeks of fieldwork in 22 universities, usually face-to-face by the TEPAV team rather than online so that the aims of the project could be explained and any queries answered immediately. They were then analysed statistically

---
[14] This may be why the report has little mention of initial teacher training or the impact of not including English in the school-leaving examination.

and examined by all three project partners. The numbers of completed questionnaires were as follows:

| English teachers | N =350 |
|---|---|
| EMI teachers | N = 64 |
| Students | N = 4320 |

- **Observation**
  The consultant observed classes in all of the universities visited. These included both language classes in preparatory schools and EMI/ESP classes in undergraduate and graduate programmes. Key elements in each lesson were identified and tabulated so that quantitative data could be derived from a qualitative process. The numbers of lessons observed were as follows:

|  | Total | Female teachers | Male teachers | Native speakers | Non-native speakers |
|---|---|---|---|---|---|
| ELT lessons | N = 49 | 43 | 6 | 9 | 40 |
| EMI/ESP lessons | N =16 | 8 | 8 | 3 | 13 |

- **Structured interviews**
  Face-to-face structured interviews were carried out in each of the universities included in the survey – both those visited by the consultant and those visited by TEPAV's External Affairs Coordinator. Institutional profiles were completed in interviews with representatives of the rectorate of each university, and departmental profiles were constructed from the director or assistants in each school or department responsible for delivering English language teaching. The numbers of profiles drawn up during the structured interviews were as follows:

|  | Total | Public universities | Foundation universities |
|---|---|---|---|
| Institutional profiles | N=21 | 12 | 9 |
| Departmental profiles | N=24 | 14 | 10 |

- **Focus groups** In each university, the consultant and, on occasions, the British Council Project Manager met with groups of English teachers to elicit their views on teaching, good practice and issues. These focus groups were conducted without directors or assistant directors being present so that teachers could speak fully and frankly. The focus groups ranged from four to 55 participants, with an average of 15. In all, 351 teachers took part in the focus groups.

- **Desk research** Extensive desk research was carried out using documents relating to higher education in Turkey in general and English-language teaching in particular. The list of documents consulted is given in the list of references attached to this report. Where necessary, translations from Turkish into English have been provided.

**Piloting** In order to validate the various research methods and instruments, a pilot was conducted at two universities (one public, one foundation) not included on the full CoHE list. As a result of this pilot, various revisions were made to both the quantitative and qualitative research instruments. Data from the pilot have been included in the findings presented in this report as far as possible.

**Limitations** While the research was carried out on a large scale, it included only 12.5 per cent of all universities in Turkey. The teachers observed and interviewed were selected by the universities themselves according to guidelines set out by the project partners.

The programme of visits and observations was intense: 22 universities in eight cities across Turkey were visited in 25 days. While this was adequate for observations, interviews and focus groups, it left little time for in depth discussion with students. In addition, the original plan did not include observations of EMI lessons and it sometimes proved difficult to add these to university visits.

**Timeline** Planning and piloting took place in February 2015. The fieldwork was carried out in March–April 2015.

## Research ethics
As far as possible, the research was carried out in accordance with the norms of educational and linguistic research ethics in Turkey and the UK. In particular, assurances were given to all individuals and institutions that the research would be confidential and anonymous. Participants were informed that the results would be shared through a publication and dissemination events with relevant stakeholders.

# 1 International context: globalisation

## 1.0 The educational revolution

In the past ten years, there has been what Graddol[15] calls an 'educational revolution' in response to the demographic, economic and technological changes that have taken place across the world. For higher education, this has led to the globalisation of universities – the transformation of universities from local or national institutions into global ones which must compete for students, staff and funding:

> The top universities are citizens of an international academic marketplace with one global academic currency, one global labour force and, increasingly, one global language, English. They are also increasingly sending their best graduates to work for multinational companies. The creation of global universities was spearheaded by the Americans; now everybody else is trying to get in on the act.[16]

Turkey has clear ambitions to 'get in on the act' as part of its drive to become one of the world's top ten economies by 2023. This ambition was set out in July 2013 at a joint CoHE-British Council Conference entitled 'Generating Knowledge, Innovation and Growth':

> "We are fully aware that we can't become one of the top ten economies in the world without a world-class university system and without world-class scientists and engineers,... We have to have smarter machines, smarter schools, smarter universities, a smarter economy and smarter companies," he [Davut Kavranoğlu, Deputy Minister of Industry, Science and Technology] said and added that universities "must play a central role in the development of Turkey and transformation into a high-tech, high-value economy."

> However, Kavranoğlu admitted in his keynote speech on 3 July that there was a need for real reform of the higher education system to be able to meet the 2023 targets. He said "We cannot expect our universities to deliver with the current university system that we have in Turkey." [17]

This quotation makes clear Turkey's need for world-class universities to contribute to its economic growth in the coming years. It also provides the context within which English is taught and used in Turkish universities, because, as will be seen, English plays an unparalleled role as the major language of academic research publication, exchange and instruction.

This section will look at how far Turkey has succeeded in creating world-class universities. In particular, it will examine the following areas:

1 University league tables
2 Research
3 The Bologna process
4 Student mobility
5 Staff mobility
6 The role of English

---
[15] Graddol 2006: 70
[16] *The Economist*, 8 September 2005, quoted by Graddol 2006: 74
[17] `World-class universities key to knowledge economy plan', *World University News* 280 [www.universityworldnews.com/article.php?story=2013011111]

## 1.1 University league tables

Various league tables ranking the world's universities have appeared in recent years, and these not only identify the top universities but have become drivers for quality and change. These league tables differ in the criteria they employ and the respect in which they are held. One of the most respected, the UK-based *Times Higher Education* ranking, indicates that Turkey has made great strides in the years since 2013:

> Turkey has had an exponential year ... It now boasts four top 200 universities with some spectacular rises in the ranks. The Middle East Technical University jumps from outside the top 200 at 85th, thanks to strong improvements in its reputation, international outlook and research impact scores. Istanbul Technical University enters the top 200 to joint 165th place and Sabancı University debuts in joint 182nd.[18]

The *Times Higher Education* rankings for 2015 include a separate table for countries classified as 'emerging economies' and again Turkey makes a strong showing, with three universities in the top ten and eight[19] in the top 100:

| Country | Count |
|---|---|
| China | 27 |
| Taiwan | 19 |
| India | 11 |
| **Turkey** | **8** |
| Russia | 7 |
| S Africa | 5 |
| Brazil | 4 |
| Thailand | 3 |
| Mexico | 2 |
| Poland | 2 |
| United Arab Emirates | 2 |
| Czech Republic | 2 |
| Chile | 2 |
| Hungary | 2 |
| Malaysia | 1 |
| Pakistan | 1 |
| Colombia | 1 |
| Morocco | 1 |

Figure 3: University rankings: Top 100–BRICS and Emerging Economies Rankings 2015 (Source: Times Higher Education Supplement: www.timeshighereducation.co.uk / world - university - rankings)

---

[18] Annual university rankings published by the *Times Higher Education Supplement*, 2015. NB The fourth Turkish university in the top 200 is Boğaziçi in 139th place (see Figure 5).
[19] METU (3rd), Boğaziçi (7th), Istanbul Technical University (8th), Sabancı (15th), Bilkent (19th), Koç (29th=), Istanbul (51st), Hacettepe (82nd).

However, Turkey's performance looks less strong when viewed from other perspectives:

- First, while Turkey has four universities in the top 200 according to the *Times Higher Education*, it has none in the top 200 listed by the QS and Shanghai tables, which are calculated according to rather different criteria (see Figure 5).
- Secondly, Turkey has fewer top-ranking universities than other emerging economies such as Mexico and South Korea in the 'MIST'[20] group of countries.
- Thirdly, Turkey's own URAP rankings include many more (76) universities but also include many more universities much lower down the rankings.

---

[20] MIST is an acronym for Mexico, Indonesia, South Korea and Turkey. The term was invented by Jim O'Neill, the Goldman Sachs economist who also invented the acronym "BRIC" for four quite different economies – Brazil, Russia, India and China. MIST pulls four more far-flung G20 countries together to describe the next tier of large "emerging economies".

These three issues can be seen in the following figure:

| RANKING | MEXICO | | | | INDONESIA | | | | SOUTH KOREA | | | | TURKEY | | | |
|---|---|---|---|---|---|---|---|---|---|---|---|---|---|---|---|---|
| Source | Urap | QS | Shan | THE | Urap | QS | Shan | THE | Urap | QS | Shan | THE | Urap | QS | Shan | THE |
| 1-99 | 0 | 0 | 0 | 0 | 0 | 0 | 0 | 0 | 1 | 3 | 0 | 3 | 0 | 0 | 0 | 1 |
| 100-199 | 1 | 1 | 0 | 0 | 0 | 0 | 0 | 0 | 3 | 3 | 1 | 1 | 0 | 0 | 0 | 3 |
| 200-299 | 0 | 4 | 1 | 0 | 0 | 0 | 0 | 0 | 2 | 2 | 4 | 1 | 0 | 0 | 0 | 1 |
| 300-399 | 0 | 4 | 0 | | 0 | 1 | 0 | | 4 | 2 | 4 | | 0 | 2 | 0 | |
| 400-499 | 1 | 2 | 1 | | 0 | 1 | 0 | | 6 | 3 | 2 | | 4 | 3 | 1 | |
| 500-599 | 0 | 0 | | | 0 | 1 | | | 4 | 5 | | | 4 | 1 | | |
| 600-699 | 0 | 0 | | | 0 | 0 | | | 3 | 6 | | | 0 | 1 | | |
| 700-799 | 1 | 0 | | | 0 | 4 | | | 4 | 0 | | | 3 | 2 | | |
| 800-899 | 0 | | | | 0 | | | | 3 | | | | 2 | | | |
| 900-999 | 1 | | | | 0 | | | | 5 | | | | 5 | | | |
| 1,000-99 | 1 | | | | 0 | | | | 2 | | | | 4 | | | |
| 1,100-99 | 1 | | | | 0 | | | | 4 | | | | 10 | | | |
| 1,200-99 | 3 | | | | 0 | | | | 1 | | | | 5 | | | |
| 1,300-99 | 0 | | | | 0 | | | | 5 | | | | 10 | | | |
| 1,400-99 | 1 | | | | 0 | | | | 1 | | | | 6 | | | |
| 1,500-99 | 0 | | | | 1 | | | | 3 | | | | 5 | | | |
| 1,600-99 | 2 | | | | 1 | | | | 0 | | | | 4 | | | |
| 1,700-99 | 1 | | | | 1 | | | | 0 | | | | 7 | | | |
| 1,800-99 | 0 | | | | 1 | | | | 0 | | | | 3 | | | |
| 1,900-99 | 0 | | | | 1 | | | | 1 | | | | 4 | | | |
| totals | 13 | 11 | 2 | 0 | 5 | 7 | 0 | 0 | 52 | 24 | 11 | 5 | 76 | 9 | 1 | 5 |

**Sources** Urap University Ranking by Academic Performance (URAP) Research Laboratory, Informatics Institute of Middle East Technical University
QS *QS World University Rankings* published by British Quacquarelli Symonds (QS).
Shan Academic Ranking of World Universities published by the Centre for World-Class Universities at Shanghai Jiao Tong University.
THE Times Higher Education World University Rankings

Figure 4: World rankings of MIST universities

It is this third issue – the large number of poorly–performing universities outside the top 1,000 – that is perhaps of most concern. Until recently, only a few of Turkey's 175 universities were listed in global league tables, so that the majority did not know how weak they were or what their weaknesses were. For this reason, since 2011 the URAP (University Ranking by Academic Performance) table of the world's top 2,000 universities has been produced annually by the Middle East Technical University, which uses nine performance indicators to calculate a global ranking, giving 'a chance for Turkish universities to monitor themselves in terms of academic performance'[21].

| University | Status | Medium of Instruction | URAP (1,000) | QS (800) | Shanghai ARWU (500) | THE (300) | SCIMAGO (1,000) |
|---|---|---|---|---|---|---|---|
| METU | Public | English | 433 | 401-10 | - | 85 | 569 |
| Boğaziçi | Public | English | 575 | 399= | - | 139 | (1,155) |
| Istanbul Technical | Public | Turkish & English | 488 | 501-50 | - | 165= | 671 |
| Sabancı | Foundation | English | (1,192) | 471-80 | - | 182= | (1,794) |
| Bilkent | Foundation | English | 860 | 399= | - | 226-50 | (1,274) |
| Koç | Foundation | English | (1,162) | 461-70 | - | - | 475 |
| Hacettepe | Public | Turkish & English | 525 | 601-50 | - | - | (1,875) |
| Istanbul | Public | Turkish & English | 489 | 601-50 | 401-50 | - | 440 |
| Ankara | Public | Turkish | 535 | 701+ | - | | 549 |
| Ege | Public | Turkish & English | 487 | | | | 582 |
| Gazi | Public | Turkish & English | 532 | | | | 522 |
| Erciyes | Foundation | Turkish & English | 791 | | | | 894 |
| Dokuz Eylül | Public | Turkish & English | 991 | | | | 907 |
| Marmara | Public | Turkish & English | 982 | | | | 984 |
| Gaziantep | Public | English | 831 | | | | (1,529) |
| Çukurova | Public | Turkish & English | 729 | | | | (1,126) |
| Süleyman Demirel | Public | Turkish & English | 760 | | | | - |
| Mersin | Public | Turkish & English | 957 | | | | (1,791=) |
| Selçuk | Public | Turkish & English | 978 | | | | 834 |
| Yıldız Technical | Public | Turkish | 987 | | | | (1,343) |
| Gaziosmanpaşa | Public | Turkish | 1,000 | | | | (1,804) |
| Atatürk | Public | Turkish | 959 | | | | 890 |
| TOTALS | Public 17 Foundation 5 | EMI 6 TMI 4 T-EMI 12 | 20 | 9 | 1 | 5 | 12 |

Figure 5: Turkey's top-ranking universities:
URAP 1,000, QS 800, Shanghai 500, THE 300, SCIMAGO 1,000

[21] Ömrüuzun F and O Alaşehir (n/d), *A National Ranking for Turkish Universities*: URAP-TR [file:///I:/URAP~%20 %20National%20Ranking%20for%20Turkish%20Universities]

The URAP rankings of the top 2,000 universities seem very valuable, but they still include only 76 of Turkey's 175 universities and they are more concerned with *identifying* areas of weakness rather than *rectifying* them. As Kavranoğlu pointed out (Section 1.0 above), reform is needed in order to rectify the situation and improve the quality of the large number of under-performing universities in Turkey, and it is worth considering the kinds of reforms that are taking place in other emerging economies in order to contrast them with the changes in the Higher Education Law proposed in Turkey.

A somewhat similar situation occurred in Russia, where there were large numbers of universities that were not included in the university rankings. In response, the government surveyed what was happening in other countries and then launched a large-scale, funded programme to transform its top universities, as described by Alexander Povalko, Deputy Minister of Education and Science:

> Project 5-100 was launched in 2013 to support the best universities in Russia, with a desire to see at least five of them enter the top 100 of the leading global university rankings by 2020. We have tried to incorporate the best from the concepts and experience of the Chinese 211 and 985 projects, the South Korean Brain Korea 21 programme, the Japanese Global 30 project, the German Excellence Initiative and many others. The best international experts in creating world-class universities were engaged to create the Project 5-100 concept.
>
> However, the ambition to reach the top of the ranking is not the primary aim of the project. The rankings serve only as important indicators, among many others, to measure university performance. Project 5-100 is a comprehensive academic excellence initiative that unites top-tier Russian universities behind the goal of deep transformation of the institutions according to the best international models and practices.
>
> This transformation has three objectives. First, we want to change the university environment, upgrading it to a world-class level by creating extensive English language communications; a large choice of international educational programmes; comfortable campus accommodation and services.
>
> Second, we want to reform our university research to join in partnership with leading international research teams and to form such teams ourselves; to increase our presence in highly-cited international research journals; to develop active collaboration between universities and business and industry; and to increase the demand for our technology transfer in the global market of innovative products.
>
> Third, we want to increase the attractiveness of our universities in order to recruit talented international faculty and students to promote our education and research, and to make the best Russian universities well known abroad.[22]

Turkey's situation is not exactly the same as Russia's: Turkey, unlike Russia, already has more than one university in the top 200 (although some seem to share some of the weaknesses identified by Povalko), but Turkey may need similar policies and investment if it is to maintain the quality of its top universities and to ensure that the quality of its other universities is enhanced so that they can contribute to national development.

---

[22] www.timeshighereductaionco.uk/world-university-rankings/2015/brics-and-emerging-economies/analysis/push-for-the-top

It will be argued throughout this report that the current 'English deficit'[23] in Turkish universities is prevalent in virtually all aspects of university activity and that it seriously undermines the quality of the universities, their ability to compete globally, and the ability to contribute to the economic development of the country.

## 1.2 Research

Research is not only the key indicator of the quality of universities, but also a key factor in national economic development. The latest Scimago research review[24] places Turkey 20th in the world rankings:

| Rank | Country |
|---|---|
| 1 | United States of America |
| 2 | China |
| 3 | United Kingdom |
| 4 | Germany |
| 5 | Japan |
| 6 | France |
| 7 | Canada |
| 8 | Italy |
| 9 | India |
| 10 | Spain |
| 11 | Australia |
| 12 | South Korea |
| 13 | Russian Federation |
| 14 | Netherlands |
| 15 | Brazil |
| 16 | Taiwan |
| 17 | Switzerland |
| 18 | Sweden |
| 19 | Poland |
| 20 | Turkey |
| 21 | Belgium |
| 22 | Israel |
| 23 | Iran |
| 24 | Austria |
| 25 | Denmark |

Figure 6: Scimago Country Research Rankings (2014)

[23] See Koru and Akesson 2011. This report was based on Turkey's performance on the English Performance Index (EPI) test; for a more detailed update revealing Turkey's English deficit profession by profession, see Education First 2014; see also Figure 2.
[24] [www.scimagojr.com/countryrank.php]; MIST rankings are Mexico 28th, Indonesia 61st, South Korea 12th, Turkey 20th

Another recent review, focusing on the Middle East[25], begins by stating that research lags behind that of the West, but also points to the 'particularly impressive progress' of Turkey and Iran, noting that Turkey produces about half of the region's research articles and reviews. Turkey has also seen a steep rise in research output, from just over 5,000 papers in 2000 to nearly 22,000 in 2009 – a rise from 0.7 per cent to 1.9 per cent of the world total.

While these figures are impressive, neither review shows the spread of the research across the universities in Turkey. However, the latest Scimago review lists only 60 Turkish universities among the world's top 5,000 research institutions, suggesting that approximately two-thirds should be classified as virtually 'research-inactive'[26]. This is a serious weakness: even low-ranking universities should have some research activity and research should inform their teaching. Such a situation requires attention, perhaps through a periodic 'research assessment exercise' (RAE) of the kind carried out in other countries.

A further question is the extent to which academic research is accessible to faculty members and students in Turkish universities. The overwhelming majority of all academic research is published in English. In recent years the number of academic journals has more than doubled and the number of non-English journals has also more than doubled, but, according to a recent survey,[27] 'English is generally considered to be the lingua franca of the scientific community. For example, roughly 80 per cent of all the journals indexed in Scopus are published in English.'

An even more important point is the extent to which this research is accessible to Turkish academics:

- As the vast majority of research in all fields is published outside Turkey and is written in English, Turkish researchers need good levels of English to access most research in their field.

- As the vast majority of research in all fields is written in English, Turkish researchers need good levels of English if their research is to be published and disseminated internationally.

  In both skills – reading academic journals and writing for peer-reviewed academic journals – Turkish academics state that their proficiency is inadequate. In the present research, academics were asked to identify which skills need improvement:

---

[25] Adams J et al (2011), *Global Research Report – Middle East*, Leeds: Thomson Reuters
[26] (www.scimagoir.com); see also Figure 5
[27] Van Weijen (2012); other estimates are higher: Barnett et al. (2012) suggest that 85 per cent of Scopus journals are published in English.

| English language skill | EMI Universities | E&TMI Universities | TMI Universities | All Universities | Rank |
|---|---|---|---|---|---|
| Writing for peer-reviewed academic journals | 1.6 | 1.5 | - | 1.6 | 3= |
| Improving my academic reading | 1.4 | 1.2 | - | 1.3 | 7 |

**Which of the following courses would you like to attend to support your teaching of English? (0 = not useful, 3 = essential)**

Figure 7: Language priorities of EMI academics (N = 64)

These figures reinforce the idea that there is an 'English deficit' in Turkish universities, and that this deficit is likely to undermine both the quantity and quality of research produced in Turkish universities and the ability of Turkish academics to access the research in their fields to support the quality of their teaching and their own research publications.

## 1.3 The Bologna process

The second main driver of university globalisation has been the Bologna process, which was originally signed by 29 countries in 1999 and which now has 49 signatories. Turkey[28] signed up in 2001, along with Croatia, Cyprus and Liechtenstein. The main aims of Bologna are European harmonisation of higher education across five main areas:

- degree structure (the three-tier bachelor, masters, doctorate system)
- recognition of degrees and study periods
- joint degrees
- social dimension – access to higher education, gender issues, lifelong learning, etc.
- quality assurance.

Turkey's motivation in signing the Bologna agreement relates to quality and internationalisation:

> Concerning higher education, modernisation and internationalisation ideas construct the basis of the reforms and explain the desire to take part in the Bologna process. The existing need for reform in the higher education system and the trust in the suggested reforms of the Bologna Process to improve the higher education system has been motivating for the participation in the process. Furthermore, being a signatory of the Bologna Process is considered important in improving the international reputation of Turkish universities, and making them more competitive in the international market.[29]

---

[28] For reviews of Turkey's adaptation to the Bologna process in general, see Westerheijden et al. (2010), Yağcı (2010), Füruzan (2012), Yakışık (2012)
[29] Westerheijden et al (2010), The Bologna Process Independent Assessment: The First Decade of Working on the European Higher Education Area, Volume 2 – Case Studies and Appendices, Chapter 6 Turkey, page 94

Turkey has generally performed well in the first three areas of the Bologna process, but has made little progress with lifelong learning.[30] All of the universities which completed institutional profiles during the fieldwork for this project stated that they were Bologna-compliant, although two said that compliance was "in progress". More than half singled out the European Credit Transfer and Accumulation System (ECTS) as evidence of their compliance, although this has not replaced the older credit system and work still needs to be done to measure credits in terms of student workload and learning outcomes.[31] Nearly all were positive about Bologna, mentioning the advantages of course documentation, learning outcomes, student participation in evaluation, international collaboration and mobility. One university said that the impact had been "not so significant" and one stated that taking 30 credits per semester was not always feasible for all students.

## 1.4 Quality assurance

The second Bologna area which has been problematic in Turkey (and which has impacts on English language teaching) is quality assurance. While initial steps have been taken to create a national quality assurance system, notably the setting up of the Commission for Academic Assessment and Quality Improvement in Higher Education (YÖDEK) in 2005, it does not fully meet the Bologna requirements[32] and this was acknowledged by the President of CoHE in 2014:

> Our (CoHE's) primary objective is to create a quality assurance system that focuses on the output of our education institutions, and not just the setting of quality standards and controlling the inputs.[33]

In the absence of a full national system, universities have either developed their own internal QA systems or have joined external/international systems. University English language departments have been particularly active: through the conference of directors of preparatory schools, DEDAK (Dil Eğitimi Değerlendirme ve Akreditasyon Kurulu) which was established in 2012, although this is still in its infancy and is not yet operational. International systems are more widespread, with schemes from the UK (Pearson Assured and BALEAP), the Council of Europe (EAQUALS) and the USA (CEA). Each of the universities visited during the fieldwork was asked about quality assurance, and the following table summarises their responses:

---

[30] During the fieldwork research for this project, only a handful of mature students were encountered in observed classes and universities stated that it is difficult to admit 'non-traditional' students because of current university entrance requirements. This is confirmed by Westerheijden et al 2010: 99, Yağcı 2010: 592
[31] Füruzan 2012: 108, Yağcı 2010: 590
[32] See Westerheijden et al 2010: 97, Yağcı 2010: 591-92
[33] Çetinsaya G (2014), 'What does the future hold for higher education?', New Statesman, 21-27 March 2014, page 11

| University type | Pearson Assured[34] | EAQUALS[35] | CEA[36] | BALEAP[37] | None |
|---|---|---|---|---|---|
| State | 4 | 0 | 1 | 0 | 8 |
| Foundation | 2 | 1 | 2 | 1 (application) | 4 |
| TOTAL | 6 | 1 | 3 | 1 | 12 |

Figure 8: Accreditation schemes used by English/Foreign language departments

As can be seen, nearly half[38] of the universities visited have been granted or are in the process of being granted external, international accreditation. The four accreditation schemes mentioned here – Pearson Assured, EAQUALS, CEA and BALEAP – have different aims and methods: Pearson Assured is available for any educational programme whereas the other three are specific to English language teaching; all schemes involve inspection but not all require classroom observation; all schemes require fees but the fees differ widely. Nevertheless, these figures suggest commendable initiative, considerable work and documentation, the meeting of international standards, and a high level of transparency.

## 1.5 Student mobility

International student mobility is one of the most visible results of the globalisation of higher education: the HE market has been growing by seven per cent a year since the late 1990s, and a 2011 study by the OECD estimated that 4.3 million students worldwide were paying US$170 billion for fees and living expenses, and that this market could grow to eight million students by 2025.[39] Competition to attract these students is fierce and Turkey has expressed its ambition to become a major player in this market.

There are three main reasons why a country would want to attract international students and, although any country is likely to have mixed motives, in most countries it is possible to identify the dominant reason:

- Quantity: Attracting large numbers of poorly-qualified international students in order to provide a revenue stream for universities and the wider economy. A good example of this in the eastern Mediterranean region is the Turkish Republic of Northern Cyprus, where international students outnumber local students by about 4 to 1.
- Quality: The quality of a country's universities attracts large numbers of highly-qualified international students, mostly to graduate programmes. The quality of the students further boosts the quality of the universities, especially as many will remain as research students or faculty. This is the model of many European

---
[34] Formerly EdExcel Assured, UK
[35] Evaluation and Accreditation of Quality in Language Services, Council of Europe
[36] Commission on English Language Program Accreditation, USA
[37] British Association of Lecturers in English for Academic Purposes, UK
[38] This compares very favourably with Turkish universities in general, where only about 25% are engaged in any external review (Westerheijden *et al* 2010: 97; Yağcı 2010: 596)
[39] Cited by *Daily Sabah*, 5 November 2014 [www.dailysabah.com/education/2014/11/05 accessed 08 February 2015]

universities such as the UK and the Netherlands.
- Ideology: A country attracts international students by generous scholarship schemes in order to promote its ideology or culture. The most obvious example of this model was the Soviet Union, which attracted over 125,000 international students per year by 1990, over ten per cent of the world's total at the time.

Although it could be argued that Turkey's policy has elements of the third model, it is usually said that there is no clear, identifiable policy when it comes to international students:

> It is not possible to say that Turkey has an effective international student policy. The growth of higher education has doubled; the number of international students has not increased by a similar amount.[40]

In recent times there has been a lot of hype in the local media and on the internet about Turkey as a hub of international higher education. For example:

> Turkey – geo-politically important, multicultural, and an Erasmus member – is catching the attention of an ever-increasing number of international students. In today's *ICEF Monitor* we speak with Miraç Özar, Director of the International Office at Özyeğin University and a key member of Turkey's collaborative effort to gain more international students at its universities. Dr. Özar fills us in on what Turkey offers international students as well as potential partnering institutions in the West. In addition, we provide an overview of Turkey's aim to become a regional hub for higher education, with a goal of hosting 100,000 students in 2015 and 150,000 students by 2020.[41]

Such reports perpetuate several misconceptions about Turkish higher education:

- Turkey attracts large numbers of international students. In fact, the numbers are relatively small.

- The students who are attracted to Turkey are truly 'international'. In fact, most come from the region, the Turkish diaspora or what one university calls 'the Ottoman hinterland'.

- Turkey is a net importer of international students. In fact, the numbers of Turkish students travelling overseas far exceed those coming to Turkey, so that Turkey is the world's fifth largest exporter of students.

- International students provide an economic boost for Turkey. Figures are difficult to obtain, but it is likely that international students are a drain on the Turkish economy.

Each of these misconceptions will be explored in more detail below.

The total numbers of international students attracted to Turkey in 2003–12 and the source countries are shown in the table below:

---

[40] Özoğlu *et al* 2012: xxv
[41] 'Turkey aims to build on recent gains to host 150,000 international students by 2020', *ICEF Monitor* [http://monitor.icef.com/2014/06 accessed 08/02/2015]

| Country | 2003 | 2004 | 2005 | 2006 | 2007 | 2008 | 2009 | 2010 | 2011 | 2012 |
|---|---|---|---|---|---|---|---|---|---|---|
| Azerbaijan | 1,299 | 1,394 | 1,506 | 1,673 | 1,953 | 2,307 | 2,739 | 3,540 | 4,257 | 7,379 |
| Turkmenistan | 1,109 | 1,083 | 1,176 | 1,342 | 1,507 | 1,793 | 2,129 | 2,929 | 4,110 | 6,136 |
| N Cyprus | 2,723 | 2,611 | 2,501 | 2,366 | 2,337 | 2,472 | 3,252 | 3,503 | 3,828 | 4,221 |
| Germany | 125 | 143 | 202 | 266 | 391 | 556 | 794 | 1,143 | 1,383 | 1,822 |
| Greece | 1,136 | 1,055 | 994 | 884 | 875 | 850 | 963 | 1,099 | 1,322 | 1,704 |
| Iran | 615 | 682 | 796 | 859 | 906 | 975 | 1,087 | 1,305 | 1,488 | 1,690 |
| Afghanistan | 181 | 220 | 321 | 362 | 472 | 581 | 737 | 812 | 1,047 | 1,679 |
| Bulgaria | 1,021 | 1,111 | 1,163 | 1,169 | 1,178 | 1,147 | 1,134 | 1,231 | 1,236 | 1,263 |
| Syria | 262 | 291 | 279 | 264 | 260 | 291 | 339 | 455 | 608 | 962 |
| Kazakhstan | 707 | 695 | 708 | 701 | 681 | 701 | 683 | 727 | 810 | 922 |
| Kyrgyzstan | 709 | 675 | 647 | 590 | 549 | 528 | 533 | 602 | 746 | 904 |
| Mongolia | 329 | 388 | 519 | 692 | 815 | 899 | 915 | 956 | 932 | 901 |
| Russia | 662 | 625 | 604 | 556 | 524 | 491 | 495 | 516 | 567 | 713 |
| Iraq | 182 | 209 | 236 | 246 | 266 | 293 | 326 | 370 | 452 | 573 |
| Macedonia | 271 | 292 | 312 | 309 | 308 | 307 | 330 | 334 | 413 | 535 |
| Nigeria | 0 | 22 | 0 | 0 | 63 | 74 | 177 | 224 | 342 | 513 |
| Albania | 513 | 532 | 561 | 545 | 533 | 499 | 502 | 482 | 492 | 507 |
| Georgia | 91 | 82 | 104 | 134 | 212 | 262 | 302 | 371 | 412 | 471 |
| Somalia | 1 | 1 | 0 | 0 | 2 | 5 | 11 | 10 | 252 | 459 |
| Palestine | 209 | 177 | 167 | 155 | 153 | 140 | 167 | 202 | 298 | 431 |
| Bosnia | 399 | 462 | 523 | 494 | 479 | 518 | 513 | 674 | 616 | 430 |
| Tajikistan | 217 | 186 | 189 | 165 | 162 | 176 | 194 | 239 | 277 | 380 |
| Indonesia | 7 | 7 | 8 | 11 | 19 | 43 | 101 | 142 | 219 | 369 |
| China | 107 | 101 | 110 | 136 | 154 | 174 | 200 | 240 | 276 | 346 |
| USA | 29 | 14 | 26 | 34 | 45 | 57 | 133 | 198 | 221 | 302 |
| Ukraine | 308 | 276 | 241 | 219 | 210 | 209 | 198 | 208 | 232 | 282 |
| Uzbekistan | 92 | 84 | 88 | 94 | 99 | 117 | 149 | 159 | 210 | 275 |
| TOTAL | 13,304 | 13,418 | 13,981 | 14,266 | 15,153 | 16,375 | 19,103 | 22,671 | 27,046 | 36,169 |

Figure 9: International Students in Turkish Universities 2003–2012
(Source: Çetinsaya 2014: 154 (totals recalculated))

While the growth rate and the annual total may look impressive, they are tiny both in global terms and even as a percentage of Turkey's university student population[42]:

| Country | No. of international students | Share of global total | Percentage of national university population |
|---|---|---|---|
| USA | 624,000 | 18.9 | 3.0 |
| UK | 336,000 | 10.1 | 15.0 |
| Germany | 246,000 | 7.3 | 12.4 |
| France | 243,000 | 7.5 | 11.2 |
| Australia | 231,000 | 7.0 | 21.0 |
| Turkey | 24,551 | 0.7 | 0.8 |

Figure 10: Statistics for international students worldwide (2010)[43]

Figure 9 shows the source countries of international students and also reveals that the majority of these students are 'regional' rather than 'international': more than 50 per cent come from the Turkic republics, the Turkish Republic of Northern Cyprus, the Turkish diaspora in Europe and Balkan countries, attracted by government grants and speaking Turkish or a related language. In particular, they are attracted by scholarships from the Büyük Öğrenci Projesi (Grand Student Project), a scheme established in 1992 after the dissolution of the Soviet Union to attract students from Turkic republics which gained independence from the USSR, and more than 20 other scholarship programmes, which together were worth US$ 96 million in 2014.[44] Despite these attractions, the quotas for foreign students at Turkish universities are not always filled[45] and as many as 40 per cent fail to graduate, returning home without their degrees for reasons of finance and difficulties with language and cultural adjustment.[46]

It seems likely that the total number of students coming from the traditional regional market is reaching its limit, and universities see future expansions in numbers as coming from elsewhere in the Middle East and Africa, areas which do not currently contribute significantly to the totals. However, Turkish-medium programmes would not be attractive to such students and consideration would have to be given to offering more English-medium courses if this market is to be tapped and the numbers of international students doubled or even quadrupled.

While Turkey ranks low in the countries attracting international students, it is one of the highest-ranking countries for exporting students. In 2013, the British Council carried out a survey of Turkish students' attitudes to international education,[47] which revealed that 95 per cent would like to study overseas, seeing it as a good way to secure future employment. The most popular

---
[42] Özcan 2011 (translated from Turkish)
[43] Universities in our fieldwork survey reported higher numbers of international students for 2014–15: 2.5 per cent in state universities and 5.85 per cent in foundation universities
[44] *Daily Sabah*, 10 July 2014
[45] *Zaman* 30 January 2011; for example, the Turkish-Africa Undergraduate Scholarship Programme is available to students from 54 African countries, yet Nigeria and Somalia are the only African countries listed in Figure 9.
[46] For difficulties of international students in Turkey, see Özoğlu et al. 2012: 3-4
[47] Shepherd 2013

destinations would be the UK (30 per cent), the USA (30 per cent) and Germany (8 per cent), and the main advantages were seen as being better educational opportunities (32 per cent), exposure to different ways of thinking and learning (25 per cent) and better employment prospects after studying (16 per cent).

While most Turkish students were unable to study overseas, mainly for reasons of finance, many do: 2011-12 totals suggest that approximately 12,000 went to the USA, 7,000 to Germany and 3,800 to the UK[48]. These figures relate specifically to those taking degrees abroad; the total number of Turkish students studying abroad is far higher, making Turkey the fifth highest student exporter in the world:

| Rank | Country | Student totals |
|---|---|---|
| 1 | China | 722,915 |
| 2 | India | 222,912 |
| 3 | South Korea | 138,601 |
| 4 | Germany | 131,781 |
| 5 | Turkey | 82,981 |

Figure 11: Top five senders of internationally-mobile HE students (2011)
(Source: New Statesman, 21-27 March 2014
(totals include exchange, language and non-credit students))

The trade in outgoing Turkish students is so lucrative that there are 300-350 recruitment agencies in Turkey. A 2013 report on the activities of these agencies gives a clearer picture of the kinds of programmes that attract Turkish students:

| Programme | Percentage |
|---|---|
| Language and summer schools | 78% |
| Masters and doctorates | 59% |
| College and undergraduate degrees | 48% |
| Certificates | 32% |
| High school | 5% |

Figure 12: Programme preferences of outgoing Turkish students
(Source: ICEF Monitor 01/10/2013 { monitor.icef.com/.../what-do-turkish-students-look-for-when-studying-abroad accessed 01/04/2015)

The final misconception is that international students bring large benefits to the Turkish economy, but for this to happen several conditions would have to change:

---
[48] Shepherd 2013: 6

- There would have to be a massive increase in the numbers of international students coming to Turkey.
- They would have to pay full-cost fees rather than receive scholarships and/or pay subsidised fees at state universities.
- The numbers of Turkish students choosing to go overseas rather than study in Turkey would have to decline as the numbers and costs of outgoing students currently exceed the numbers and income of incoming students.

The costs of international student mobility are high, with fees averaging around US$10,000 per student per year and total expenses doubling this figure.[49] The revenue currently received by Turkey for incoming international students is difficult to determine because low fees and scholarships given to students by the government and various foundations limit the net income, but one estimate puts the current figure at US$1.75 billion, rising to US$7 billion in 2023 if Turkey can succeed in attracting 180,000 international students per year.[50] Estimates for the current costs of outgoing Turkish students are as high as US$1.5 billion per year.[51]

## 1.6 Staff mobility

In a recent CoHE report (Çetinsaya, 2014) it was stated that Turkish universities need 45,000 more academic staff if they are to reach the OECD average student-staff ratio of 16 to 1. This represents a massive 32 per cent increase from the current total of 141,000.[52] The same report revealed that, at present, 45 per cent of academics (öğretim elemanı) hold PhD degrees and concludes that there is a shortfall of 20,000 fully-qualified faculty in Turkish universities.[53] Although the academics in the research for the current project reported a rather higher figure (67.2 per cent), these figures go some way towards explaining the issues with university quality and research output already touched on in this chapter.

The same CoHE report goes on to discuss the low numbers of foreign academic staff in Turkish universities, suggesting that some of the shortfall in academic staff could be made up by recruiting foreign staff in a process often referred to as a 'brain gain':

> Whereas there were 1,700[54] international lecturers/instructors in Turkey in 2012, the number exceeded 2,800 according to the statistics of April 2014 of YÖK. Although the number of international staff has gradually increased, the total proportion of all international staff has reached only 1.9%. It is lower in comparison with other developing countries and does not match the aims of Turkey to reach international levels. ...
>
> When we compare the distribution of the number of international lecturers/instructors in state

---

[49] Cited by Daily Sabah, 5 November 2014 [http://www.dailysabah.com/education/ 2014/11/05 accessed 08 February 2015
[50] Turkey's target: 100,000 international students by 2020 [http://skilledmigrationresearch.blogspot.co.uk/ 2012/03 accessed 08 February 2015]
[51] http://www.dunya.com/ekonomi/ekonomi-diger/44-bin-yabanci-universiteliden-1-8-milyar-dolar-egitim-geliri-212059h.htm, accessed 22 April 2015
[52] Çetinsaya 2014, summarised on official Study in Turkey website [http://studyinturkey.com/content/sub/report_claims_turkish_universities, accessed 22 April 2015]
[53] Çetinsaya 2014: 129
[54] i.e. 1.2 per cent

and private universities, considering the fact that there were approximately 1,700 international staff in 2012, private universities are much more likely to attract international staff. This may result from the fact that there are many departments which provide education in foreign languages and are preparatory classes. Private universities provide better conditions for international staff and this causes international staff to choose private universities. It is known that international staff are generally hired as foreign language instructors.[55]

The CoHE report also identifies some of the programmes for recruiting more international staff. These suggestions make it clear that this recruitment may not be easy and are in contrast with reports from a few years ago which confidently talked of Turkish 'brain rain', suggesting that there was a "boom in foreign academics".[56] One particularly valuable method of attracting international staff that is not mentioned by the CoHE report is to attract more international PhD students and then to offer them employment as academics when they graduate.

Outward mobility must also be considered and other statistics suggest that there is an annual 'brain drain', with more academics leaving Turkey than arriving from overseas:

| Year | Incoming staff | Outgoing staff |
|---|---|---|
| 2004-05 | 218 | 339 |
| 2005-06 | 440 | 581 |
| 2006-07 | 666 | 1,378 |
| 2007-08 | 931 | 1,904 |
| 2008-09 | 1,184 | 1,595 |
| 2009-10 | 1,321 | 1,740 |
| 2010-11 | 1,649 | 2,159 |
| 2011-12 | 2,058 | 2,642 |
| 2012-13 | 2,570 | 3,886 |
| TOTAL | 11,037 | 16,224 |

Figure 13: Staff mobility in Turkey (2004-2012) (Source: Çetinsaya 2014:158)

Other indicators of concerns about staff mobility are the fact that over one quarter of all the international staff (440 of 1,703) are concentrated in just eight universities and over 40 per cent in 25 universities[57], and the low percentage of international collaborative research in Turkey[58].

## 1.7 Findings and recommendations

The findings of Section 1 are summarised in the following paragraphs and the implications for English language teaching are made clear. Each finding is then followed by a recommendation. (See also Chapter 6 for findings and recommendations.)

---
[55] Çetinsaya 2014: 156 (translated from Turkish)
[56] 'World's academic "brain drain" becomes Turkey's "brain rain"', Hürriyet Daily News, 2 April 2011 [http://www.hurriyetdailynews.com.default, accessed 02/04/2011]
[57] Çetinsaya 2014: 158
[58] Only 16 per cent of research in Turkish universities has linkage to other countries, compared with around 40 per cent in Jordan, Saudi Arabia and Egypt (Adams et al 2011: 9)

**1.7.1 University league tables** Turkey has made impressive progress in increasing both the quantity and quality of its universities in recent years, with several universities now in the top 200 in the world according to the THES and URAP league tables. However, continued efforts will be needed to maintain these rankings and to promote more universities, and for this improved levels of English proficiency will be needed to ensure that quality research can be published and disseminated, and that both academics and graduate students can access the full range of research in their fields to support their teaching and further research.

Turkey also has 100 universities which are outside the top 2,000 in the world according to the URAP ratings, and the quality of these institutions needs to be improved. Even if the majority of these are Turkish-medium universities, the English proficiency levels of their staff will need to be improved so that they can improve their qualifications and access English-language resources in their field in order to inform their teaching.

**Recommendation** *Academic English language provision should be improved at all levels – preparatory, undergraduate, graduate and staff – as part of a government-backed programme to upgrade Turkish universities so that they can improve their standings in league tables. Elements of this programme might include the setting of English-language standards for students, English teachers and academics, more and more targeted professional training for EMI academics and English teachers, and more relevant English curricula at preparatory, undergraduate and graduate levels.*

*For universities which fall outside the world's top 1,000, English programmes should be introduced to improve the qualifications of staff and enable them to access the resources in their field in order to inform their teaching.*

**1.7.2 Research** As has already been stated, the English proficiency levels of academics in top-ranking universities need to be improved in order for them to carry out their research and (if required) their teaching through the medium of English.

It is recognised that lower-ranking universities will continue to produce little or no research, but the academics in these institutions will still need good levels of English proficiency to access research to support their teaching.

**Recommendation** *English for academics (EfA) courses should be offered to academic staff to raise their proficiency levels so that they can carry out research, especially international collaborative research, and disseminate their findings.*

**1.7.3 Bologna process** The Bologna process does not require the use of English, but its use has been encouraged as it makes it easier for students to carry out all or part of their studies in another country under various exchange programmes.[59] It also has the effect of increasing the use of English as a lingua franca for university documentation and communication as there is inevitably more contact between universities in different countries.

**Recommendation** *All English departments should be fully compliant with the requirements of the Bologna process and should assist the university administration with all language-related requirements. An ESP course for administrative staff should be available.*

**1.7.4 Quality assurance** In order to encourage a culture of quality teaching and research in Turkish universities, quality assurance schemes that are compliant with Bologna requirements will need to be extended or introduced. Such schemes, including schemes that are specific to English language teaching, are already in use in half of the universities surveyed.

**Recommendation** *All English departments and schools of foreign languages should aim to qualify for national and international accreditation through a recognised quality assurance scheme, preferably an international accreditation scheme specialising in language teaching.*

**1.7.5 Student mobility - inward** Turkey has more than doubled the numbers of international students in its universities in recent years, but these have mainly come from the Turkic region or diaspora, where it can be expected that they can follow Turkish-medium classes. If these numbers are to be doubled or quadrupled in line with the government's plans, international students will have to come from a wider area outside the Turkic countries, and these students are unlikely to be able or willing to speak Turkish at the level required for university study. The logic of this is that not only will more English-medium programmes have to be offered, but English will be required to support a range of other measures needed to promote internationalisation and academic mobility:[60]

- revise the current legislation and develop future policy to promote international collaboration and mobility
- improve physical and human capacity in HEIs to support international academic co-operation and mobility
- expand the range of programmes available and promote the provision of education at the internationally-recognised high standards for all levels of HE
- promote international research initiatives and activities
- develop promotion and marketing strategies to attract and recruit more international students worldwide.

---

[59] See Graddol 2006: 74
[60] See Özcan 2011

**Recommendation** *Consideration should be given to recruiting high-quality international students from the wider world, and for providing the necessary EMI programmes and resources at both undergraduate and, especially, graduate levels. Incidentally, more international students might reduce Turkish students' passiveness, lack of motivation and increase their need to learn English for a communicative purpose.*

**1.7.6 Student mobility - outward** Turkish students wish to study overseas for a variety of reasons, either as part of their programme at a Turkish institution or to gain academic qualifications at a university in another country. In both areas, English language limitations influence mobility: the uptake of Erasmus opportunities has been restricted by poor English proficiency[61] and those wishing to take a full degree overseas will usually have to undertake an English course in order to meet the necessary entry requirements.[62]

**Recommendation** *English language provision at Turkish universities should be raised to international standards so that Turkish students can access international degree programmes and compete equally in the world market for academic courses and jobs. (For suggestions, see recommendations in Chapters 3 and 4.)*

**1.7.7 Staff mobility** Many of Turkey's academics lack PhD degrees and many of these will want to study for their doctorates overseas, with the most popular destinations being the USA and UK. They will need good scores in IELTS, TOEFL or similar examinations in order to undertake graduate study overseas.

Turkey has very low levels of international academic staff and joint research programmes. If these levels are to be raised, improved levels of English will be needed. In particular, more English-medium programmes, especially at graduate level, will be necessary if more international academics are to be attracted to Turkish universities.

**Recommendation** *Academic staff should be offered ESP courses for academics (EfA) so that they can travel overseas for academic programmes, events, courses and employment.*

*More graduate-level EMI programmes should be introduced in order to encourage international staff and research co-operation. International staff are more likely to be able to contribute to EMI graduate programmes, and international research is greatly facilitated by having a common language for work and publication.*

---

[61] Westerheijden *et al* 2010: 96
[62] See Top 10 Reasons Turkish Students Study Abroad [www.edufairs.net/top-10-reasons-turkish-students-study-abroad accessed 07/04/2015]

# 2 National context: language of instruction

## 2.0 Introduction

Turkey has seen a rapid growth in the number of universities and the total has more than doubled in the past 15 years:

|            | 2001 | 2003 | 2006 | 2007 | 2008 | 2009 | 2010 | 2011 | 2012 | 2015[63] |
|------------|------|------|------|------|------|------|------|------|------|----------|
| Public     | 53   | 53   | 68   | 85   | 94   | 94   | 102  | 103  | 103  | 104      |
| Foundation | 23   | 24   | 25   | 30   | 36   | 45   | 54   | 62   | 65   | 71       |
| TOTAL      | 76   | 77   | 93   | 115  | 130  | 139  | 156  | 165  | 168  | 175      |

Figure 14: Numbers of Turkish universities (2001-2015)

The current total is made up of both state and foundation universities, and each university may use Turkish, English or mixed Turkish-English as its medium of instruction. While a particular language is not mandated or forbidden, the whole question of which language(s) should be used for instruction is 'an important part of the planning of education policy in Turkey'[64].

It is difficult to give precise figures for the numbers of universities using particular languages because languages of instruction may be mixed in various ways, and also because universities do not always make the position clear in their publicity materials. However, an indication of the situation can be gained from looking at the 24 universities visited during the pilot and fieldwork for this project:

| Status     | English medium | Turkish medium | Mixed Turkish-English medium | TOTAL |
|------------|----------------|----------------|------------------------------|-------|
| State      | 3              | 2              | 9                            | 14    |
| Foundation | 5              | 1              | 4                            | 10    |
| TOTAL      | 8              | 3              | 13                           | 24    |

Figure 15: Medium of instruction

The picture that emerges here is that State universities are now mostly mixed Turkish-English medium (T-EMI), with small but equal numbers of English (EMI) and Turkish (TMI) medium universities. Foundation universities are also mostly T-EMI but with no TMI universities. However, there are reasons to be cautious of these figures: it would seem that most of the T-EMI universities are mostly Turkish medium, but have introduced around 30 per cent of their classes in English in order to preserve access to their preparatory schools. One also needs to be cautious about what 'English' actually means in T-EMI classes, as it can be very different from university to university, programme to programme (see Chapter 5 below).

---

[63] Eight new foundation universities were approved by parliament 02 May 2015: Ibn Haldun University, Turkey International Islam, Science and Technology University, İstinye University, Bandırma Sept 17th University, İskenderun Technical University, Alanya Alaaddin Keykubat University, AKEV University, Rumeli University. All are apparently TMI.
[64] Kırkgöz 2009: 81; see also Başıbek et al. 2013: 1821.

This chapter will look at the various options and try to determine the advantages and disadvantages of each in the Turkish context. It will also distinguish undergraduate from graduate programmes. The structure of the chapter, therefore, is as follows:

1 English medium (EMI) undergraduate programmes
2 Turkish medium (TMI) undergraduate programmes
3 Mixed Turkish-English medium (T-EMI) undergraduate programmes
4 Graduate programmes
5 Findings and recommendations

## 2.1 English medium (EMI) undergraduate programmes

There has been a long history of using English as a medium of instruction in Turkey, dating back to the founding of Robert College (now Boğaziçi University) in 1863:

> Robert College was founded in 1863 in Istanbul, Turkey, by Dr. Cyrus Hamlin, an educator, inventor, technician, architect and builder, and Mr. Christopher Rheinlander Robert, a well-known philanthropist and a wealthy merchant from New York. ... A curriculum was drawn up, and Hamlin insisted that English should be the language of instruction. [65]

This lead was followed with the establishment of Middle East Technical University in 1956 and Turkey's first foundation university, Bilkent, in 1984.

The academic advantages of adopting English as the medium of instruction are often said to be[66]:

- providing full access to academic textbooks and research papers in English
- facilitating international research publication and dissemination
- facilitating international academic mobility for students and staff
- attracting international staff.

All of these advantages relate more to graduate study and academic staff than to undergraduate programmes in Turkish universities and, while they may have been applicable in 1863, 1956 or even 1984, they are much less convincing in 2015, when adequate textbooks in Turkish are available in most subjects, and undergraduate students are not required to read, write or publish research papers in English. While English was previously seen as a gateway to knowledge, in the context of modern Turkey it can be a barrier. This conclusion was underlined when, in the course of the fieldwork for this project, two undergraduate courses were observed on writing introductions to research papers and using referencing conventions in academic papers. When the lecturer and the students were asked if these were actually requirements for academic students in the universities concerned, the responses were negative, reinforcing the requirement for a curriculum based on a thorough needs

---
[65] Boğaziçi University website [boun.edu.tr/index_eng.html accessed 13/03/2015]
[66] See Coleman 2006: 5-7 for a survey review of both the advantages and disadvantages of EMI in higher education

analysis. At all universities visited, staff were asked whether their undergraduate programmes could be taught in Turkish and in only two subjects – computer engineering[67] and, for different reasons, tourism – did staff and students say that EMI was academically or vocationally essential, but further research would be needed to confirm this conclusion.

There is clearly a need for an analysis of what English language tasks are actually required on undergraduate EMI programmes, but the fieldwork visits revealed that only one university had carried out a full and recent needs analysis and that no preparatory school curricula were currently based on a needs analysis (although one university has recently carried out a full needs analysis and is currently analysing the results). However, a full needs analysis was carried out at Çukurova University (Kırkgöz 2009, following West 1994) and the results are given below:

| Rank | Academic task requirements | Always | | Often | | Sometimes | | Never | |
|---|---|---|---|---|---|---|---|---|---|
| | | No. | % | No. | % | No. | % | No. | % |
| 1 | Answering exam questions | 190 | 86.3 | 18 | 8.1 | 12 | 5.6 | - | - |
| 2 | Following the lecturer's instructions during lessons | 176 | 80 | 34 | 15.4 | 10 | 4.6 | - | - |
| 3 | Note-taking in a lecture and summary writing using notes | 165 | 75 | 15 | 6.8 | 33 | 15 | 7 | 3.2 |
| 4 | Summarising a text | 160 | 72.7 | 8 | 3.6 | 40 | 18.1 | 12 | 5.6 |
| 5 | Reading various texts on a topic to express one's opinion | 154 | 70 | 22 | 10 | 39 | 17.8 | 5 | 2.2 |
| 6 | Guessing the meanings of unfamiliar words from context | 148 | 67.2 | 44 | 20 | 8 | 3.6 | 20 | 9.2 |
| 7 | Writing a project on a topic incorporating ideas from various sources | 138 | 62.7 | 74 | 33.6 | 3 | 1.3 | 5 | 2.4 |
| 8 | Asking and answering questions during lessons | 66 | 30 | 114 | 51.8 | 28 | 12.7 | 12 | 5.5 |
| 9 | Expressing opinions during class discussions | 44 | 20 | 134 | 60.9 | 26 | 11.8 | 14 | 7.3 |
| 10 | Report writing | 22 | 10 | 80 | 36.3 | 34 | 16.5 | 82 | 37.2 |

Figure 16: Needs analysis: students' responses on required academic tasks (N=220) (Source: Kırkgöz 2009: 87)

---

[67] It should be noted that some universities do teach Computer Engineering in Turkish, although 'Computer Engineering is a relatively recent discipline in Turkey, computer-related terms are largely derived from English, and … Turkish equivalent of some technical terms is rather unclear' (Kırkgöz 2014: 453)

These figures reveal that the students' needs are actually internal course requirements rather than short or medium-term academic needs, confirming that they do not need to use their English for academic reading of textbooks or journals or writing academic papers. In other words, if the programme were to be delivered in Turkish, all of these 'requirements' would disappear.

These findings were confirmed by the research in the present project, where students, English teachers and academics all confirmed that students were motivated more by longer-term occupational, academic and recreational reasons than by their immediate EMI needs:

| Reason | Students (N=4,320) | | English teachers (N=350) | | Academics (N=64) | |
|---|---|---|---|---|---|---|
| | Rank | Score | Rank | Score | Rank | Score |
| To meet employers' demands for good English | 1 | 2.6 | 3= | 2.1 | 1 | 2.5 |
| To study in other countries | 2 | 2.5 | 1 | 2.3 | 2 | 2.4 |
| To travel to other countries | 3 | 2.4 | 2 | 2.2 | 3= | 2.2 |
| To pass professional exams | 4= | 2.3 | 3= | 2.1 | 5= | 2.1 |
| To pass international English language exams | 4= | 2.3 | 3= | 2.1 | 3= | 2.2 |
| To follow university lectures/classes | 6= | 2.1 | 6= | 2.0 | 5= | 2.1 |
| To write university papers/essays | 6= | 2.1 | 8= | 1.5 | 10 | 1.5 |
| To read academic books/journals | 6= | 2.1 | 8= | 1.5 | 8= | 1.7 |
| To take part in university discussions | 9= | 1.7 | 8= | 1.5 | 8= | 1.7 |
| To use the internet/computer | 19= | 1.7 | 6= | 2.0 | 7 | 1.8 |

Figure 17: Students' reasons for learning English
(Responses were given on a scale from 0 (not important) – 3 (most important of all))

These figures confirm that English is mostly needed for occupational reasons which could be dealt with more efficiently and more specifically by a dedicated English course in Year 4 (see Chapter 3 of this report) or for study abroad, which very few students do (again, see Chapter 3).

EMI also has serious disadvantages for Turkish universities. The disadvantages of EMI in general have been well documented[68]:

---

[68] Smith 2004 cited by Coleman 2006: 6-7; see also Başıbek et al 2013: 1821

- inadequate language skills and the need for training of indigenous staff and students
- ideological objections arising from a perceived threat to cultural identity and the status of the native language as a language of science
- unwillingness or inability of local staff to teach through English
- the lack of availability on the international market of sufficient anglophone subject specialists
- the inability of recruited native speaker tutors to adapt to non-native speaking students
- inadequate proficiency of incoming international students in the host language
- organisational problems and administrative infrastructure
- lack of interest from local students
- loss of confidence and failure to adapt among local students
- lack of critical mass of international students
- lack of cultural integration of international students
- financing the teaching of international students where no fees exist
- financing for international students from poorer countries where fees do exist
- uniformity and availability of teaching materials
- equity of assessment for native and non-native English speakers.

While all of these might apply to Turkey, several seem to be particularly relevant as during the fieldwork, three limitations on universities' ability to deliver effective EMI programmes were encountered:

- The poor English language skills of students, even after the preparatory year. The levels of English of students graduating from secondary schools are unlikely to improve in the short term; indeed, teachers complained in focus groups that levels have declined in recent years. This inevitably means that EMI universities are competing for fewer and fewer students with good English proficiency, and the competition will become stronger and the levels of students will become weaker as more EMI programmes are introduced. The general perception that EMI programmes attract better students may currently be true[69], but these students are unlikely to have good English skills. This is confirmed by the low numbers of students currently exempted from preparatory schools because they already have good English – in some universities in the current survey the number of exempted students was zero.
- The poor motivation of students, especially during the preparatory year.
- The poor standards of English of lecturers in academic departments, which put severe constraints on the number and quality of EMI programmes they could deliver. In several universities there was evidence from focus groups of academics who were required to teach a course in English simply because they were among the few whose English was good enough, regardless of whether the students wanted or needed the course.

Some of these issues will be discussed further in Chapter 5 which considers the

---

[69] See Çokgezen 2014: 8, where 'the minimum entrance score for economics departments using English language instruction is about 37 points higher than for the Turkish language only departments'.

classroom practicalities and methodology of delivering EMI programmes and some suggested remedies for the problems that were observed.

A further problem with EMI in general and in Turkey in particular is the way in which English-medium instruction interferes with the learning process. While EMI students list some advantages of EMI – enhancing English language skills, access to primary sources in English, better employment prospects and keeping up with global developments[70] – they listed five major shortcomings of EMI, all of which contrast with corresponding advantages of TMI[71]:

| Disadvantages of EMI | Advantages of TMI |
| --- | --- |
| Difficulty of understanding disciplinary knowledge | Easier comprehension of disciplinary knowledge |
| Difficulty of understanding specific details of disciplinary knowledge | More detailed acquisition of disciplinary knowledge |
| Disciplinary knowledge retained only in the short-term memory and likely to be forgotten soon. | Longer retention of disciplinary knowledge |
| Time-consuming nature of EMI | Faster access to knowledge |
| Limited ability to participate in lecture discussion or ask/answer questions | Enhanced productivity in written and spoken modes of communication. |

All of these disadvantages of EMI apply directly to the acquisition of disciplinary knowledge and illustrate the extent to which English is a barrier to learning. These limitations have been widely explored in Turkey in recent years in a number of studies, all of which have come to similar conclusions. This research has been summarised by Kırkgöz (2014: 446):

> The issue of MI and the questions related to effective learning of one's disciplinary knowledge constitute an important part of the current debates in Turkey. Kılıçkaya (2006) reports the perceptions of the Turkish instructors teaching content courses in EMI with regard to the use of English as MI. The results of the survey administered to instructors in eight universities offering EMI showed that the majority of the instructors preferred TMI over EMI on the grounds that EMI makes subject learning more difficult for students. Sert (2008) surveyed student and lecturer perceptions of the effectiveness of the use of English/Turkish in the acquisition of disciplinary knowledge in three Turkish universities offering EMI. Although EMI was found to be effective in language skill development, the research suggests that EMI fails to convey the academic content effectively. In another study, Collins (2010) investigated students' and instructors' attitudes to EMI at a private university in Turkey. Her findings revealed that, while most instructors favoured EMI, only 41% of the students agreed that English should be used as the MI. Concerning the impact of EMI on students' learning, most students contend that studying in English lowered their success rate. Likewise, most instructors strongly agreed that EMI decreased students' creativity, detrimentally affecting their self-confidence.

As a final and conclusive piece of evidence, the performances of two groups of students on the same computer examination were compared and the results

---
[70] Kırkgöz 2014: 449–50
[71] Kırkgöz 2014: 449–56

showed that the TMI students outperformed EMI students by 56.66% on the same course[72].

## 2.2 Turkish medium (TMI) undergraduate programmes
The advantages of EMI are in many ways the disadvantages of TMI:

| Advantages of EMI | Disadvantages of TMI |
|---|---|
| Providing full access to academic textbooks and research papers in English. | Inhibiting access to academic textbooks and research papers in English. |
| Facilitating international research publication and dissemination. | Restricting international research publication and dissemination. |
| Facilitating international academic mobility for students and staff. | Restricting international academic mobility for students and staff. |
| Attracting international staff. | Failing to attract international staff. |

However, it should be noted that the disadvantages of TMI apply mainly to graduate rather than undergraduate study, or to academic staff rather than students, especially Turkish students. It may also be noted that some of the disadvantages of EMI are good indicators of many of the advantages of TMI:

| Disadvantages of EMI | Advantages of TMI |
|---|---|
| Inadequate language skills and the need for training of indigenous staff and students. | Adequate language skills and no need for training of indigenous staff and students. |
| Ideological objections arising from a perceived threat to cultural identity and the status of the native language as a language of science. | No ideological objections arising from a perceived threat to cultural identity and the status of the native language as a language of science. |
| Unwillingness or inability of local staff to teach through English. | Willingness and ability of local staff to teach through Turkish. |
| Lack of interest from local students. | Improved interest from local students. |
| Loss of confidence and failure to adapt among local students. | No loss of confidence or need to adapt among local students. |

The first and third of these advantages of TMI seem self-evident, and no direct evidence of the second was encountered, in either its positive (ideological support for TMI) or negative (ideological opposition to EMI). However, a lot of anecdotal support was found for improved interest from students because of TMI, even to the point where some EMI academics complained that they were 'blackmailed' into giving their EMI lessons in Turkish by students who

---
[72] Kırkgöz 2014: 455

threatened to give them poor feedback if they insisted on giving their lectures in English. Also observed lessons repeatedly revealed students who lacked the confidence to contribute to class discussion in EMI lessons, an observation that echoes a comment from an EMI lecturer at Çukurova University:

> I would like to have interactive [EMI] lectures. When I ask a question there is always silence in the class. I am sure students have something to express but they feel reluctant to speak, feeling afraid to make mistakes.[73]

In order to determine the advantages and disadvantages of English and Turkish as mediums of instruction, a questionnaire was given to students and EMI lecturers[74]. The table below gives the results in rank order for students from EMI, TMI and T-EMI universities, and places these beside the results from academics, so that comparisons can be drawn:

| Questionnaire item | Students (N = 4,320) | | | | | Academics (N = 64) | |
|---|---|---|---|---|---|---|---|
| | EMI | T-EMI | EMI | Average/ Rank | | Average/ Rank | |
| Lecturing in Turkish allows the lesson to progress faster than lecturing in English. | 2.6 | 3.1 | 3.1 | 2.9 | 1 | 2.3 | 3= |
| The Turkish government should raise the status of the Turkish language in society. | 2.6 | 2.9 | 2.9 | 2.8 | 2 | 2.1 | 8= |
| Lecturing in Turkish produces a better classroom atmosphere than lecturing in English. | 2.5 | 2.9 | 2.9 | 2.7 | 3 | 1.8 | 11= |
| Lecturing in Turkish allows a teacher to go deeper into the content of the lesson than lecturing in English. | 2.5 | 2.9 | 2.9 | 2.7 | 4 | 1.8 | 11= |
| It is easier to set examination questions using English than using Turkish. | 2.5 | 2.8 | 2.8 | 2.7 | 5 | 2.2 | 6= |
| Learning Turkish well will benefit the learning of English. | 2.4 | 2.6 | 2.6 | 2.5 | 6 | 2.3 | 3= |
| Resources for learning, e.g. textbooks and reference books, are more plentiful in English than Turkish. | 2.6 | 2.2 | 2.0 | 2.3 | 7 | 3.3 | 1 |
| The greatest problem of using Turkish as the medium of instruction is the need to translate a lot of specialist terms. | 2.3 | 2.3 | 2.4 | 2.3 | 8 | 2.1 | 8= |
| Lecturing in Turkish can bolster students' interest more than lecturing in English. | 2.1 | 2.4 | 2.4 | 2.3 | 9 | 2.2 | 6= |
| I support adopting Turkish medium at the university where I study. | 2.6 | 1.9 | 1.7 | 2.2 | 10 | 1.1 | 16= |
| The education department should provide universities that adopt Turkish medium with more resources for teaching. | 2.0 | 2.2 | 2.2 | 2.1 | 11 | 2.1 | 8= |
| English as the medium of instruction leads to poorer student intake. | 1.9 | 2.2 | 2.1 | 2.1 | 12 | 1.4 | 13 |

---

[73] Kırkgöz 2009: 90
[74] The questionnaire was shortened from one given by Kılıçkaya (2006), which was itself based on one used in Hong Kong by Tung, Lam and Tsang (1997). The same questionnaire was used by Başıbek et al. 2013.

| | | | | | | | |
|---|---|---|---|---|---|---|---|
| Even studying every subject in Turkish will not help students with poor academic performance. | 1.8 | 1.9 | 1.9 | 1.9 | 13 | 2.5 | 2 |
| It is easier to teach non-language subjects (e.g. Geography, Mathematics) in English than in Turkish. | 2.0 | 1.7 | 1.5 | 1.8 | 14 | 2.3 | 3= |
| Undergraduate courses should be taught in Turkish but postgraduate courses should be taught in English. | 1.5 | 1.8 | 1.7 | 1.7 | 15 | 1.3 | 14= |
| All university courses should be taught in Turkish but special English courses should be provided for those who then go on to graduate courses abroad. | 1.4 | 1.8 | 2.1 | 1.6 | 16 | 1.3 | 14= |
| Parents are the major obstacle in the promotion of Turkish-medium education. | 1.3 | 1.2 | 1.2 | 1.3 | 17 | 1.1 | 16= |

Figure 18: Evaluating university teaching through Turkish and English (Responses on a scale of 0 (never) – 4 (always)) [75]

Several tentative conclusions can be drawn from these statistics. There seems to be fairly strong support for TMI courses from students, but rather weaker support from EMI lecturers. Students believe that they make faster progress, enjoy a better classroom atmosphere and go deeper into the subject when learning through Turkish. Lecturers find that TMI makes their lectures more interesting. Interestingly, there is stronger support the use of Turkish from EMI students than from TMI students. Both students and lecturers felt that more TMI would raise the status of Turkish in society.

These statistics support the two main findings from other countries[76] – that EMI can slow down learning (and this seems to be more likely where students' overall level of English proficiency is weak) and that courses in the mother tongue are more efficient[77].

## 2.3 Mixed medium (T-EMI) undergraduate programmes

A recent development in Turkish universities has been the adoption of mixed-medium instruction. This can take two forms: horizontal or vertical. 'Horizontal programmes' are parallel programmes which are offered in both English and Turkish, so that students can complete their undergraduate studies in one language or the other:

**English-medium programme**
(medicine, economics, engineering, etc.)

**Turkish-medium programme**
(medicine, economics, engineering, etc.)

---
[75] Broadly similar results are given by Başıbek et al. 2013: 1822.
[76] See Dearden 2014
[77] See Dearden 2014: 15 for a brief summary of issues with EMI at Turkish universities

The horizontal approach has been adopted by many European universities – the ECTS system ensures that the content, study budget, assignments and assessment of the two programmes are parallel and similar, and, ideally, a student could attend lectures on either or both courses. Horizontal programmes of this kind are offered by several Turkish universities.

'Vertical programmes' are where the two languages are used side-by-side, typically in a 70 per cent TMI to 30 per cent EMI ratio[78] :

There was clear support for mixed-medium undergraduate teaching, but the statistics do not allow us to distinguish between the two models. However, it was apparent from observation that horizontal programmes could be said to offer the best of both worlds; vertical programmes offer the worst of both worlds. In vertical lectures it was observed that students were more likely to be demotivated, passive, asleep, absent and to have poor understanding of the content. Students adopted various strategies for compensating for their lack of comprehension and language proficiency: asking and answering questions in Turkish, whispering explanations to each other, spending time looking up the content of the lecture on TMI sources, demanding summaries or even the whole lecture in Turkish, etc. All the arguments against EMI (see Section 2.1 above) apply to T-EMI. Interviews with academics also confirmed the lack of support for T-EMI teaching: deans and faculty stated that they could not see any academic advantages to this approach and expressed their conviction that it had been adopted for administrative reasons rather than academic advantage. The counter-arguments – that T-EMI exposes students to more academic English and that Turkish is not suitable as an academic or scientific language – were not supported by observations or interviews. Alternative ways to provide exposure to relevant English will be suggested in Chapter 3.

## 2.4 Graduate programmes

By international standards, Turkey has an average proportion of graduate students. Figures for 2013-14 suggest that the total for masters and doctoral students is 8.9 per cent, compared with 8–10 per cent in the UK:

| Status | Undergraduates | | Masters students | | PhD students | | Total students |
|---|---|---|---|---|---|---|---|
| State universities | 3,139,516 | 92.2% | 206,014 | 6% | 60,227 | 1.8% | 3,405,757 |
| Foundation universities | 231,172 | 78.8% | 56,738 | 19.3% | 5,637 | 1.9% | 293,547 |
| TOTALS | 3,370,688 | 91.1% | 262,752 | 7.1% | 65,864 | 1.8% | 3,699,304 |

Figure 19: Numbers and percentages of students in Turkish universities (2013–14)[79]

---

[78] All mixed-medium programmes seem to be TMI courses with some EMI; no examples of the opposite situation were found.
[79] Istatistik.yok.gov.tr (March 2014), quoted by YÖK 2014: 16

It is difficult to determine what the proportion of the EMI graduate programmes is, partly because doctoral programmes in particular tend to be negotiated between student and supervisor[80]. However, the number of internationally-advertised EMI master's programmes is known to be 173, placing Turkey 20th in the world rankings:

| Rank | Country | Number of EMI Masters |
|---|---|---|
| 1 | United Kingdom | 11,665 |
| 2 | United States | 4,541 |
| 3 | Germany | 1,935 |
| 4 | France | 1,275 |
| 5 | Netherlands | 1,068 |
| 6 | Spain | 903 |
| 7 | Ireland | 779 |
| 8 | Sweden | 737 |
| 9 | Switzerland | 677 |
| 10 | Italy | 577 |
| 11 | Austria | 548 |
| 12 | Australia | 479 |
| 13 | Canada | 390 |
| 14 | Belgium | 384 |
| 15 | Denmark | 376 |
| 16 | Portugal | 306 |
| 17 | Finland | 278 |
| 18 | Norway | 238 |
| 19 | Poland | 196 |
| 20 | Turkey | 173 |
| 21 | Greece | 166 |
| 22 | Romania | 152 |
| 23 | Hungary | 141 |
| 24 | Republic of Cyprus | 128 |
| 25 | Czech Republic | 121 |

Figure 20: Number of EMI master's programmes (2015)[81]

---

[80] One still encounters anomalous situations: at one university an international PhD student negotiated to do his research in English, published a series of articles in peer-reviewed journals in English, but was still required to write his thesis in Turkish because of inflexible university regulations.
[81] Master Worldwide – mastersPortal.eu [www.mastersportal.eu/countries accessed 24 April 2015]. These statistics should be treated as indicative – there are many EMI masters programmes which are not registered on the Masters Worldwide website.

While Turkey seems to outperform other MIST nations, the country's total of 173 EMI master's programmes suggests an average of only one programme per university, but in fact only 15 universities list EMI masters and 133 (77 per cent) of these EMI programmes are offered by just five institutions, all of them foundation universities. In the fieldwork for this project, there was stronger support from students for teaching graduate programmes in English than in Turkish:

|  | EMI universities | T-EMI universities | TMI universities | All universities |
|---|---|---|---|---|
| Graduate courses should be taught in English | 1.5 | 1.4 | 1.3 | 1.4 |
| Graduate courses should be taught in Turkish | 0.9 | 1.1 | 1.2 | 1.0 |

Figure 21: Student opinions on graduate programmes (N= 4320)[82]

The conclusions would seem to be that relatively few master's degrees are currently being offered through the medium of English. There is room for considerable expansion of provision and fairly strong support from students. If Turkey really means to attract large numbers of international students in the coming years, offering more EMI masters would seem to be a good place to start.

## 2.5 Findings and recommendations

The findings of Section 2 are summarised in the following paragraphs and the implications for English language teaching are made clear. Each finding is then followed by a recommendation. (See also Chapter 6 for key findings and recommendations.)

**2.5.1 English medium (EMI) undergraduate programmes** At the present time, when students entering university generally have low levels of English proficiency, EMI undergraduate programmes offer few advantages for the majority of students and may actually reduce the pace and efficiency of learning.

**Recommendation** *Consideration should be given to limiting the numbers of 100 per cent EMI programmes until such time as there are adequate numbers of students and staff with appropriate levels of English-language proficiency[83]. At present the language proficiency levels of both students and staff are inadequate to support current levels of EMI programmes.*

**2.5.2 Turkish medium (TMI) undergraduate programmes** Undergraduate programmes through TMI offer academic advantages to most students. Although it has to be acknowledged that more academic resources are available in English than in Turkish, adequate textbooks and other materials are available

---
[82] Students were asked to respond on a 0 (= none) – 2 (= all) scale
[83] See Shatrova 2014: 154: `At the same time, almost every participant believed that "there is no need to teach everybody. I am tired of teaching the people who strongly object to it. Teaching should be selective and flexible". In other words, the Turkish instructors thought it would be beneficial to change the approach and reconsider the policies of English as the language of instruction.'

for students in Turkish for almost all subjects with the possible exception of computer engineering.[84]

**Recommendation** *Consideration should be given to prioritising TMI programmes and to improving the resources available to TMI programmes.*

**2.5.3 Mixed medium (T-EMI) undergraduate programmes** Horizontal or parallel programmes delivered through English and Turkish are already offered in some Turkish universities and follow a model that is becoming more common elsewhere in Europe. Parallel programmes that permit students to access lectures in either or both languages offer particular advantages.

The English components of vertical programmes which deliver most of the course in Turkish with a minimum of 30 per cent in English seem largely ineffective, with low levels of engagement and comprehension. These are always Turkish-medium courses with some EMI lectures, and so the English language proficiency levels of the majority of students are likely to be low. There is little evidence that T-EMI courses actually improve students' English in any way, and they almost certainly impede their academic progress. The purpose of these mixed-medium programmes is open to question: are they really provided to assist students' academic capabilities or merely for administrative reasons?

**Recommendation** *The current policy of increasing numbers of vertical mixed-medium (T-EMI) programmes delivered partly in Turkish and partly in English should be reviewed with a view to phasing them out. In their place, parallel programmes delivering the same content in Turkish and in English should gradually be introduced, when they can be justified and supported by the English proficiency levels of EMI academic staff and students.*

**2.5.4 Graduate programmes** In contrast to developments in other countries, Turkey offers relatively few EMI master's degrees, and, of these, the majority are offered by just 15 foundation universities. An expansion of EMI graduate programmes would seem to offer several advantages:

- an improvement in the overall quality of the programmes as students would have access to more research resources
- an improvement in the quantity and quality of the research produced and published by universities with EMI graduate programmes
- improvements in the world rankings of Turkish universities
- attracting more international students
- attracting more international staff.

**Recommendation** *Consideration should be given to expanding the number of EMI graduate programmes in order to improve the quality of graduate teaching and research, and to attract more truly international students and academic staff.*

---
[84] Teaching staff would have to access English-medium resources to support their teaching in most fields

# 3 Institutional context: language teaching programmes

## 3.0 Introduction

English is traditionally taught at Turkish universities in a one-year preparatory school teaching 'foundation', 'basic' or 'access' English, and then through language support classes during undergraduate programmes. The first preparatory school was established at Boğaziçi University (then Robert College) in 1958 and METU followed in the early 1960s, using audio-lingual textbooks and weekly quizzes purchased from Robert College[85]. In 1996 each university providing EMI programmes was required to establish a preparatory school to offer a one-year English for Academic Purposes (EAP) curriculum[86] and in 2001-2002 this requirement was extended to TMI universities.[87] A recent reversal of this policy, whereby preparatory school English is available only to those taking courses with at least 30 per cent EMI, has led many universities to incorporate more EMI in what were formally purely TMI courses so that their preparatory school programmes can be retained.

It is in the light of this long history of preparatory school English and changing policies that the current review of English programmes is being carried out. It will look at four principal issues:

1 Provision and eligibility
2 Distribution of ELT programmes
3 Curriculum
4 Quality

## 3.1 Provision and eligibility

Currently all EMI and T-EMI students are eligible for a preparatory school English programme unless they are exempted because they perform well in the university's entrance test or they have a certain score in an accepted international English language exam. In practice, this means that between 5 and 25 per cent of students can pass straight to their undergraduate courses, while the majority undertake the foundation year in the preparatory school. In most universities, students can 'graduate' from preparatory school at the end of each semester if they achieve a certain score on an in-house exam, although in a few universities they move on to a 'pre-faculty' course for the rest of the academic year. Most universities have provision for repeat programmes for those who fail at the end of the preparatory year, so that some students can remain in a preparatory school for two or more years.

This situation was largely confirmed during the fieldwork: in all the universities visited, the preparatory year was compulsory for all EMI and T-EMI programmes. Most universities responded that the preparatory year was not available for TMI students, but a few said that it was 'voluntary' or 'at the request of the

---

[85] Prof Dr Hüsnü Enginarlar (interview)
[86] Kırkgöz 2009: 81
[87] Doğancay-Aktuna and Kızıltepe 2005: 253

department'. However, this situation was not confirmed by students during the fieldwork, where more than 80 per cent claimed that the preparatory year was compulsory for TMI students and over 90 per cent of all TMI students claimed that they were attending or had attended a preparatory year:

| (N = 4320) | | EMI | T-EMI | TMI | average |
|---|---|---|---|---|---|
| Is the prep year compulsory in your university? | Yes | 91.9% | 86.5% | 66.8% | 88.0% |
| | No | 8.1% | 13.5% | 33.2% | 12.0% |
| Did you attend/are you attending the prep year? | Yes | 89.9% | 90.1% | 92.2% | 90.1% |
| | No | 10.1% | 9.9% | 7.8% | 9.9% |

Figure 22: Preparatory school attendance

When discussing preparatory school provision all the English teachers' focus groups repeatedly stressed three points: the low level of most of the entrants, their poor motivation and the fact that preparatory school programmes are usually compulsory, at least for EMI students.

**3.1.1 Language proficiency level** The current university entrance system takes little or no account of English-language proficiency and admits students who have weak language proficiency to EMI universities and programmes. One consequence of this system is that all students taking the preparatory year are, by definition, weak at English. This situation is well-documented[88] and cannot be expected to change until there is large-scale reform and upgrading of high-school English teaching – something that is likely to take a generation. Many teachers stressed that this situation has got worse in recent years because of changes in teaching at Anatolian High Schools[89]. The questionnaire completed during the fieldwork research showed levels on entry to the preparatory school were estimated at levels A1-A1+ on the CEFR scale:

| (N = 350) | EMI | T-EMI | TMI | average |
|---|---|---|---|---|
| English level on entry to the preparatory year | 1.48 (A1+) | 1.28 (A1) | 1.15 (A1) | 1.35 (A1+) |
| English level on entry to a bachelor course | 2.16 (B1) | 2.01 (B1) | 1.84 (A2) | 2.06 (B1) |

Figure 23: Teachers' estimates of students' language levels

Given the low entry levels of most students (and the other factors discussed below), it is virtually impossible to raise levels to the target level of B2 in eight months. This, however, is not always understood and English teachers feel they are often blamed by academics and departments for not achieving the impossible[90].

---

[88] e.g. Vale et al 2013
[89] Approximately 50 per cent of the students in our survey graduated from Anatolian high schools (N=4320)
[90] It is notoriously difficult to estimate the number of hours required to move from one CEFR level to another but guidelines from the Association of Language Testers of Europe suggest a minimum of 500 hours tuition, depending on circumstances – motivation, context, etc. (quoted @ kaj.upol.cz). Turkey is not a member of ALTE.

**3.1.2 Motivation** Poor motivation was the second point stressed repeatedly. Suggested reasons for the poor motivation were students' view that the preparatory year was a 'holiday' after all their work passing the university entrance exams in their last year at school, the immature outlook of the students, their desire to just get on with their university studies and their failure to see the relevance of English to their studies or their lives at this stage in their careers. Students, however, claim that their motivation for learning English is high:

| (N = 4320) | EMI | T-EMI | TMI | average |
|---|---|---|---|---|
| For further study | 1.9 | 1.8 | 1.8 | 1.8 |
| For international travel | 1.8 | 1.8 | 1.8 | 1.8 |
| For employment | 1.9 | 1.8 | 1.7 | 1.8 |

Figure 24: Students' motivation claims[91]

Students' claims were rarely substantiated in lesson observations: their lack of motivation was evident in the lack of engagement in the lessons and problems of attendance which universities reported. To compensate, teachers tried hard to generate intrinsic motivation by delivering lessons which were potentially interactive and relevant to students' teenage interests.

It is also possible that both students and teachers are right: the students are motivated to learn English in the long term (all of the responses in Figure 24 relate to the long-term). In fact, in answer to another question during the fieldwork, students claimed that lack of motivation was a major reason limiting their progress, and this was confirmed by teachers:

| | Teachers' ranking (N = 350) | Students' ranking (N=4320) |
|---|---|---|
| Poor motivation | 1= | 3= |
| Lack of interest in English | 1= | 9= |
| Inadequate practice in speaking/listening | 3= | 2 |
| Large classes | 3= | 5= |
| Late start in learning English | 5= | 3= |
| Few chances to meet native speakers | 5= | 1 |
| Unsuitable materials | 7 | 7= |
| Not enough time for study | 8= | 7= |
| Unsuitable teaching | 8= | 5= |
| Poor resources for learning | 10 | 9= |

Figure 25: Factors affecting progress in English

---

[91] Students responded on a 0 (not important) – 2 (very important) scale

These conflicting results – Figure 24 suggesting that students are motivated to learn English but Figure 25 confirming that they are not – suggest a conflict between long - and short - term motives: students may realise that in the long-term they will need English for employment, further study and travel, but in the short term they are not motivated by 30–35 hours of English during the preparatory year, trying (as one student said) to learn the present perfect for the sixth time[92].

Motivation is in many ways the central issue as, without motivation, little learning will take place. This has been recognised in a number of studies about ELT in preparatory schools in Turkey in recent years.[93] All of these reach the same conclusions as those from the present survey:

- The majority of students (96 per cent in one study) acknowledge that they want to learn English for longer-term occupational reasons rather than shorter-term academic needs.
- Learning through English rather than Turkish reduces both the rate and depth of academic learning.

These points are best summed up by Kırkgöz (2005: 118)

> The overall impression of the students based on the findings from the survey is of a group with a mixed but mainly instrumental orientation towards long-term (post study) goals, and with a fairly positive assessment about their English, both in respect to their specific purposes and especially their general English language skills. In spite of this, the process of EME is seen as problematic for them, and they are especially concerned about the impact EME has on their learning academic subject matter....
> The students in the present study are motivated primarily by the long term benefits and opportunities knowing English may bring in a country that is experiencing economic development. Not surprisingly, owing to EME, the students experience a number of difficulties. Thus, there is a tension between the long-term advantages and short-term difficulties.

Another demotivating factor, suggested by 'unsuitable materials' in Figure 23, is that the curriculum is not of apparent relevance either to their longer-term occupational needs or to their academic fields of study. This factor is confirmed by Kırkgöz (2009):

> A general feeling regarding both the students' written comments and interview data showed that most students (93.5%) perceived a gap between the requirements of [undergraduate] disciplinary courses and what they were taught at CFL (Centre for Foreign Languages = preparatory school). While feeling that the EAP curriculum had been beneficial in language skills development, survey respondents articulated what had been lacking, as indicated by the following statements:

> *Here (referring to her department) we learn disciplinary English but there (at CFL) we learned daily English. There is a big difference between the two. When we started our department we did not see much relevance of what we had studied before.*[94]

---

[92] See Vale et al 2013: 17
[93] See Kırkgöz Y (2005 & 2009), Bektaş-Çetinkaya (2012), Başaran S and F Hayta (2013), Tokoz Göktepe (2014), Shatrova (2014)
[94] Kırkgöz 2009: 88

One could, of course, argue that a more relevant, needs-based curriculum would be more motivating, but the problem is that students do not see what they do and do not need until they reach their undergraduate programmes, i.e. after preparatory school. The implications are that a) more English should be taught in parallel to the students' undergraduate studies rather than before them, and b) the curriculum should be more relevant. These two factors will be discussed further in the following sections.

**3.1.3 Compulsion** Preparatory school classes are usually compulsory but non-credit-bearing. Teachers frequently complained that students felt they were at the preparatory school because they had to be, rather than because they needed or wanted to be, and students echoed this view in their comments on the questionnaire. All universities enforce a rigid attendance requirement, and failure rates because of inadequate attendance reach ten percent in some universities.

In some universities the preparatory year is voluntary, at least for some students, and these institutions report how successful this seems. It could be objected that making the preparatory year optional would undermine standards of English or encourage students to regard the preparatory year as a vacation. Some universities have overcome these problems by replacing compulsion with a powerful incentive: requiring students to pass either an international exam or a rigorous exit proficiency test aligned with the CEFR at the end of the year, and making it known that those who fail to meet this requirement will be redirected to a TMI programme or a TMI university elsewhere.

## 3.2 Distribution of English language programmes

The distribution of English language classes across the years and stages of academic study varies considerably, but there is a general pattern–provision declines as a student progresses through the university. Of the 24 universities visited during the pilot and fieldwork for the present project, the distribution was as follows (eligibility, varies according to whether a student is following a TMI, T-EMI or EMI programme):

| Year /stage of study | No. (N=24) | Percentage |
| --- | --- | --- |
| Prep School | 24 | 100% |
| Undergraduate 1 | 23 | 96% |
| Undergraduate 2 | 15 | 63% |
| Undergraduate 3 | 12 | 50% |
| Undergraduate 4 | 10 | 42% |
| Graduate | 8 | 33% |

Figure 26: Distribution of English language classes

As was seen in Section 3.1, students' motivation for English is at its weakest in the preparatory year, when they have little idea of what English is actually required of them as undergraduates. However, as undergraduates progress through their studies, the level of language support actually declines. There would seem to be a strong argument for improving motivation by redistributing these classes and offering more support (with a more relevant curriculum) throughout a student's undergraduate career in parallel to their specialist classes. Whether these classes should be compulsory or elective would depend on the medium of instruction – compulsory for EMI programmes and elective for TMI programmes.

The lack of provision for graduate students is a matter of some concern, for graduate students, regardless of medium of instruction, have a greater need for independent access to primary sources in English, and those following courses in universities requiring or permitting the submission of dissertations and theses in English have particular needs[95]. The provision that is offered by eight of the universities surveyed is varied and limited, with only five offering full support programmes for graduate students. In two of the universities visited there are special preparatory programmes for graduate students, who spent up to six months as teaching assistants and improving their English, and this is the sort of programme that could be expanded and formalised[96].

## 3.3 Curriculum

In the visits to universities five kinds of English language curriculum were encountered:

- **English for General Purposes (EGP)** General English consists of everyday social English, covering all four skills, but with no particular application to study or work. The advantage is that teachers will have been trained to teach EGP; the disadvantage is that students will have been trying to learn EGP while at school and may feel that it is repetitive and irrelevant.
- **English for General Academic Purposes (EGAP)** EGAP is academic English designed to teach the skills required for academic study but with no application to any particular field or study. The advantage is that students may find it of some relevance, but may also feel that it does not apply to their particular field. Another disadvantage is that teachers may not have been trained to teach EGAP[97].
- **Mixed EGP-EGAP** Many institutions stated that they teach a mix of EGP and EGAP, usually EGP in semester 1 of the preparatory year followed by EGAP in semester 2, or EGP to beginners and EGAP to pre-intermediate or intermediate students.
- **English for Specific Academic Purposes (ESAP)** ESAP refers to EAP that is applied to a particular field, e.g. English for architects, economists, dentists,

---
[95] Some universities permit submission in either language, but some still insist on a particular language, regardless of choice or suitability. This seems to be out of step with international practice.
[96] However, focus groups often stated that TAs tended to use Turkish rather than English when assisting on EMI programmes.
[97] In our survey, 64 per cent of teachers at EMI institutions claim that they did have training in EAP/ESP; only 37 of those at TMI universities claimed to have EAP/ESP training (N=51). However, 'developing my EAP/ESP teaching skills' was the number one choice for further training by English teachers, suggesting that their skills in this area are felt to be deficient (see Figure 32).

etc. The advantage is that students feel it is relevant to their studies; the disadvantage is that there are usually no published teaching materials for ESAP and teachers may feel that they lack the specialist background that they feel is needed.
- **English for Occupational Purposes (EOP)** EOP covers work-related language skills such as business telephone calls, writing business e-mails and letters, making presentations, reading business reports, etc. The advantage is that students may find EOP especially relevant as they near graduation and start looking for jobs; the disadvantage is that universities may not regard it as strictly academic.

All five types of English teaching were encountered during the fieldwork, with different types of curriculum being used at different stages in a student's academic career:

| Year | EGP | EGP- EGAP | EGAP | ESAP | EOP |
|---|---|---|---|---|---|
| Prep year | 11 | 9 | 3 | 1 | 0[98] |
| Year 1 | 1 | 1 | 16 | 6 | 0 |
| Year 2 | 0 | 1 | 8 | 6 | 0 |
| Year 3 | 0 | 0 | 5 | 7 | 0 |
| Year 4 | 0 | 0 | 4 | 6 | 1 |
| graduate | 0 | 0 | 8 | 0 | 0 |

Figure 27: Types of ELT curriculum in Turkish universities (N=24)

These figures are largely confirmed by the teachers' questionnaire:

| (N=350) | EMI | T-EMI | TMI | average |
|---|---|---|---|---|
| General English (EGP) | 41.5% | 41.5% | 42.5% | 41.5% |
| General Academic English (EGAP) | 24.5% | 13.5% | 23.5% | 19.5% |
| Narrow Academic English (ESAP) | 10.7% | 14.5% | 5.0% | 12.6% |

Figure 28: Percentage of time spent of different types of ELT curriculum

The main issue with any ELT curriculum at university is relevance and there are two ways of establishing relevance. One is a needs analysis and, as has already been stated, few universities have carried out a recent needs analysis to develop their ELT curriculum[99,100]. The other way is to ask students how useful they feel their English classes are. Overall, the usefulness of classes was perceived to be fairly low:

---
[98] These figures are based on universities' departmental profiles. In reality ESAP was encountered in one university's preparatory year.
[99] Needs analysis was ranked 5= on teachers' training requirements (see Figure 32).
[100] See Aykel and Özek (2010) and Kırkgöz(2009) for needs analyses carried out at Turkish universities

| (N=4320) | EMI | T-EMI | TMI | average |
|---|---|---|---|---|
| Preparatory year | 2.0 | 1.6 | 1.5 | 1.8 |
| Graduate courses | 1.7 | 1.7 | 1.7 | 1.7 |
| Undergraduate courses | 1.7 | 1.5 | 1.2 | 1.6 |

Figure 29: Students' perceptions of the usefulness of ELT classes[101]

These findings suggest that English classes are rated only 'quite useful' and confirm those of Kırkgöz (2009). It is worth quoting one of her students' comments on the relevance of the writing component of their EGAP course:

> EAP writing activities should deal with the materials closer to university level classes. I did not find the content of the programme academically interesting. We were asked to write short essays on general topics. When I started my department I encountered many difficulties in producing writings as required by lecturers. I wish I had more challenging writing tasks, such as research oriented projects.[102]

This quotation makes clear the irrelevance of the writing tasks (typical of those observed during observations for this project) and their demotivating effect. It is also interesting that the student mentions one way to make the task more relevant and interesting – project work. There are other ways in which EGAP courses could be made more relevant and motivating, and these ways will be discussed further in Chapter 4.

The relevance of graduate ELT programmes varied: some universities put graduate students on the undergraduates' preparatory course, while one university mounts a special preparatory course for graduate students. Two universities offer special support for thesis preparation and one has an academic writing centre. Two universities offer ad hoc support for graduate students, apparently on an individual basis.

One university offers an optional EOP course in the fourth year for students who realise the importance of English for job applications. The course covers job-related skills like internet searches for vacancies, letters of application and job interviews, as well as report writing, e-mails, presentations and uses of technology.

### 3.4 Quality

In this section various quality issues are brought together. These relate to programmes and teaching in general - assessment and standards, quality assurance, appraisal, continuing professional development (CPD) and the status of teachers. Classroom-related issues are dealt with in Chapter 4.

**3.4.1 Assessment and standards** Most universities claimed that their programmes, course materials and teaching objectives were related to the

---
[101] Respondents answered on a 0 (= no use) to 3 (= very useful) scale.
[102] Kırkgöz 2009: 89; for more on projects, see Section 4.7.

Common European Framework of Reference (CEFR), and this was certainly the case with the level descriptions of programmes and the teaching materials used. However, there has to be some concern over the attainment of standards. Most universities state that they are aiming to get their students to CEFR level B2, but in many cases it is acknowledged that this frequently slips to B1+ and the teachers' survey (see Figure 23) suggested that their estimate was that the average is only B1. If true - and classroom observation of under graduate lessons suggests that it may well be - this represents a serious slippage which would explain the complaints from undergraduate departments that students' English proficiency levels are frequently inadequate. In other words, standards are often not being maintained.

A second concern is how levels are assessed. In some cases international examinations are used for the exit proficiency test, either IELTS or institutional TOEFL. In all other cases in-house tests are used and the quality of these is extremely variable: some universities have invested heavily in training members of their testing units but others seem to be much less professional[103]. The general situation is well summed up by Dearden (2014:15):

> Students are required to undertake an English language course intended to bring them to a level at which they can operate through EMI. It is only after successfully passing the end-of-year test that students may commence their chosen field of study. Respondents in the study reported that tests are often written in-house by individual universities with little standardisation and that university teachers are not convinced that the preparatory year adequately prepares students for EMI study.

There are two main issues: the coverage of the tests and their quality as assessment instruments. Our survey of English teachers revealed that exit tests at the end of the preparatory year usually cover only a limited range of language skills:

| (N-350) | EMI | T-EMI | TMI | average |
|---|---|---|---|---|
| Reading skills | 95.4% | 98.8% | 100% | 97.4% |
| Writing skills | 95.4% | 96.4% | 92.6% | 95.6% |
| Listening skills | 90.1% | 88.5% | 88.9% | 89.2% |
| Grammar/language system | 81.6% | 92.1% | 100% | 88.1% |
| Speaking skills | 78.3% | 82.4% | 59.3% | 78.8% |
| Objective multiple-choice test | 55.9% | 73.3% | 85.2% | 66.6% |

Figure 30: Skills assessed in the preparatory school exit test

Figure 30 confirms the findings of interviews with directors and heads of department that only reading and writing are included in the majority of exit tests and that other skills may be omitted. This not only means that there will be a poor washback effect on teaching and learning (whatever is not tested

---

[103] Further training in assessment/testing was ranked as teachers' 2= training need (see Figure 32)

will not be learned and may not even be taught), but it will also undermine the standards that the universities are trying to attain.

The other concern is the quality of the tests themselves. How can anyone have any certainty that they assess at the level they are intended to? How does anyone know that they are measuring at the same level year on year? These are issues that need to be addressed and, indeed, have been addressed at some universities, which should be encouraged to share their experience and expertise.

Furthermore, teachers in one foundation university claimed that they were pressured by management to inflate exit exam marks to allow students to 'pass' and move on to their undergraduate studies. This practice is fairly common in other countries where there are preparatory schools but only one example of this practice was encountered in the current project. Nevertheless, this example further emphasises the need for rigorous testing and ethical standards.

**3.4.2 Quality assurance** It has already been noted (see Section 1.4) that around half of the English/Foreign language departments of the universities surveyed have adopted international quality assurance schemes – CEA, EAQALS, Pearson Assured or BALEAP. It needs to be stressed here that quality assurance schemes are not just indicators of professionalism for purposes of outside accreditation or student recruitment, but are factors that affect standards of teaching and assessment at all stages of the teaching/learning cycle. It is also important that all aspects of the quality assurance process are transparent and disseminated to teachers and students. A range of situations in relation to quality assurance was found: in more than half of the universities surveyed there was no apparent QA process or no complete system; in the best there was external accreditation and this was incorporated in a 'quality manual' available to both staff and students. Directors and heads of department stressed the advantages: evidence of quality, conformity with Bologna, setting of professional standards, and student and staff recruitment.

**3.4.3 Appraisal** Although nearly half of the universities visited were signed up to quality assurance schemes, only two were able to produce evidence of formal teacher appraisal schemes during structured interviews with directors/heads of department. Teacher appraisal – internal and external – is normally part of any quality assurance scheme and both (as well as assessment by students) are 'promoted' by the YÖDEK scheme[104]. The importance of teacher appraisal was stressed by one teacher at a university in Ankara following an observation class:

> There is no appraisal here! How do the management know if I am a good teacher? I prepare my lessons carefully and I try to teach good lessons, but no one ever checks on this. I could teach bad lessons with no preparation and get my salary in just the same way. No one would know!

Teacher appraisal is typically seen as a top-down process but in recent years

---

[104] See Westerheijden et al. 2010: 97

appraisal schemes have come to be seen as diagnostic and developmental rather than judgemental. Modern systems usually include the teacher's own reflective evaluation as well as feedback from students[105] and colleagues. This approach is reflected in the following description[106], which is offered here as an example of good practice from a Turkish university:

> Each source of feedback shall count towards the overall performance rating in the following proportions:
>
> 25 % Appraiser
> 20 % Appraiser
> 20 % Class observation feedback
> 20 % Preparatory class coordinator
> 10 % Staff feedback from colleagues
>  5 % Student feedback

**3.4.4 Continuing Professional Development (CPD)** CPD is another component of quality assurance and an essential component of any HEI. More than 75 per cent of the departments visited during the fieldwork included a CPD or teacher development unit as part of the departmental structure and most of these reported active programmes including internal and external workshops, visits to conferences in Turkey and abroad, visiting experts and support for higher degrees. However, the teachers' questionnaire confirmed that in around 20 per cent of the universities surveyed there was no effective departmental CPD available:

| (N=350) | EMI | T-EMI | TMI | average |
| --- | --- | --- | --- | --- |
| More than once a year | 44.4% | 48.4% | 22.2% | 44.6% |
| Once a year | 11.8% | 9.9% | 7.4% | 10.6% |
| Less than once a year | 13.7% | 13.7% | 14.8% | 13.8% |
| Never | 20.3% | 19.9% | 18.5% | 19.9% |
| Other | 3.9% | 3.7% | 33.3% | 6.2% |

Figure 31: Availability of Continuing Professional Development (CPD)

These figures were largely confirmed by another question in the survey, with 81.7 per cent of teachers (79.3 per cent in EMI institutions, 83 per cent of T-EMI and 87.2 per cent of TMI institutions) saying that they had attended a training course or event in the past year. Nevertheless, the situation is worrying and one that needs to be addressed in those universities where CPD is currently neglected or unavailable.

Teachers were also asked what their main training needs are. Unlike other countries, where language proficiency usually tops the list, English improvement came bottom and the main needs were felt to be professional development,

---

[105] A Bologna requirement; see Yağcı 2010: 595-97 for discussion of compliance in Turkey.
[106] For another example, see Murdoch (2000).

particularly in areas relating to the teaching of EAP/ESP:

| Rank | Training need | EMI | T-EMI | TMI | Average |
|---|---|---|---|---|---|
| 1 | Developing my EAP/ESP skills | 2.1 | 2.2 | 2.1 | 2.1 |
| 2= | EAP/ESP materials development | 2.0 | 2.1 | 2.1 | 2.0 |
| 2= | Using ITC/computers in my class | 1.9 | 2.0 | 1.9 | 2.0 |
| 2= | Language assessment/testing | 1.9 | 2.0 | 2.1 | 2.0 |
| 5= | EAP/ESP needs analysis/course design | 1.9 | 1.9 | 2.3 | 1.9 |
| 5= | EAP/ESP materials evaluation and selection | 1.8 | 1.9 | 2.0 | 1.9 |
| 5= | Developing EGP methodology skills | 1.7 | 2.0 | 1.8 | 1.9 |
| 8 | ELT management | 1.7 | 1.8 | 1.7 | 1.8 |
| 9 | Teaching large classes | 1.5 | 1.7 | 1.7 | 1.6 |
| 10= | Lesson planning | 1.4 | 1.6 | 1.6 | 1.5 |
| 10= | Developing my English language proficiency | 1.4 | 1.5 | 1.4 | 1.5 |

Figure 32: Teachers' training needs (N=350)
(Respondents answered on a 0 (= not useful) to 3 (= essential) scale)

The findings summarised in Figure 32 have already been referred to earlier in this report and there will be further discussion in Chapter 4.

**3.4.5 Teacher status** English teachers at universities around the world have often had low status. The problem was identified as long ago as 1984:

> Service English staff will tend to be employed on the lowest teaching grades – indeed, they may have specially low grades, such as "instructor" created just for them![107]

The term 'instructor' is used in all universities in Turkey and it does indicate a lower status than that given to academic faculty members. Instructors realise that this status frees them from the research requirement of academics and many are happy with this. However, many (59.6 per cent of the 350 English teachers surveyed) have pursued higher degrees and carried out practical research into aspects of language teaching, usually using classroom data from their own teaching. In some universities these instructors are eligible for promotion to full academic status, but in others, it seems, they are not.

In two of the universities surveyed the regulations require that the head of department/director must be a full member of the academic faculty and this occasionally leads to situations where directors are appointed who have

---
[107] Swales 1984: 11, based on his experience in the Middle East and the UK. For a more recent survey confirming this position, see Jordan 2002.

little knowledge or experience of the field under their control. This would be regarded as anomalous in any other field in any university in Turkey or any other European country, as important decisions could not be informed by professional or academic knowledge or experience. During one visit to a high-ranking university, for example, it became apparent that the director had no knowledge of the Common European Framework of Reference for Languages (CEFR), the standard used throughout Turkey, Europe and, increasingly, other countries.

## 3.5 Findings and recommendations

The findings of Section 3 are summarised in the following paragraphs and the implications for English language teaching are made clear. These are followed by detailed recommendations.

**3.5.1 Provision and eligibility** Preparatory school English language classes are currently provided for all EMI students. Changes in regulations would have meant that TMI students were no longer eligible for preparatory school, but many universities have introduced mixed-medium T-EMI programmes in order to retain preparatory school provision for students whose programmes are largely delivered through TMI.

**Recommendation** *It is recommended that preparatory school English programmes should normally be restricted to students entering 100 per cent EMI programmes and that there should be no preparatory school provision for TMI programmes. Elective EGAP programmes should be introduced for TMI programmes at undergraduate level.*

**3.5.1.1 Language proficiency level** The English language proficiency levels of most students entering preparatory school are very low, largely because of historic shortcomings in high schools which will take a generation to rectify. Students' English language proficiency does not seem to be taken much into account when they are accepted for an EMI university course, and this has a knock-on effect throughout the preparatory school programme.

**Recommendation** *An English language proficiency level should be established for selection for EMI programmes and students should not be allocated places on such programmes unless they can meet this standard, and cannot enter such programmes until they can reach the specified standard as verified by a valid examination in all language skills.*

**3.5.1.2 Motivation** Most students in preparatory school suffer from poor motivation.

**Recommendation** *Ways should be explored of improving motivation on preparatory school courses through more interactive techniques in lessons and* *more relevant curricula (see 3.5.3).*

**3.5.1.3 Compulsion** In most institutions preparatory classes are compulsory but non-credit-bearing for EMI and T-EMI students.

**Recommendation** *Preparatory school classes should be voluntary, even for EMI students, as one way of improving motivation and student autonomy.*

**3.5.2 Distribution of language programmes** English language classes in universities are concentrated at the front end, with intensive courses during the preparatory year and then very few classes during a student's undergraduate years. In most universities there is little or no provision for graduate students.

**Recommendation** *There should be credit-bearing EGAP and ESAP courses throughout all four years of the undergraduate programme so that students receive language support throughout their EMI studies and can continue to improve their proficiency levels. There should also be full language support built in to all graduate programmes, based on need.*

**3.5.3 Curriculum** The curriculum in most universities is English for General Purposes (EGP), with some English for General Academic Purposes (EGAP) in some universities. The curriculum on undergraduate programmes is again mostly EGAP, with few attempts to devise needs-based programmes which are more closely aligned with students' academic disciplines. Only one university provides a course in English for Occupational Purposes (EOP) in the fourth year, when students are applying for jobs which may require English.

**Recommendation** *The preparatory school curriculum should shift away from EGP towards EGAP and critical thinking, and ways should be found to personalise the EGAP curriculum so that it is more relevant to students' discipline interests. Undergraduate programmes should focus on EGAP and, wherever possible, ESAP, in order to improve motivation. Graduate English support programmes should offer a wide range of EAP skills and thesis writing.*

**3.5.4 Quality**

**3.5.4.1 Assessment and standards** Most language tests and examinations used by universities are developed in-house and most are of variable quality and skills coverage. Exit standards in particular are frequently not assessed reliably, with the result that many students enter undergraduate programmes without having reached a satisfactory level in all four skills of reading, writing, listening and speaking[108].

**Recommendation** *Universities with established examination procedures and models should share their expertise and even actual tests with other universities,*

---

[108] Assessment of languages in higher education in Turkey is a matter of both importance and concern, and a further, fuller survey is needed to establish the complete picture.

*as in some cases at present and in the past. Tests should be valid and rigorous, sampling the full range of language skills at agreed levels.*

**3.5.4.2 Quality assurance** While quality assurance and accreditation schemes have been adopted in many universities, there are also many which do not have adequate or even any such provision.

**Recommendation** *All English departments and schools of foreign languages should apply to a quality assurance scheme, preferably an international accreditation scheme specialising in language teaching.*

**3.5.4.3 Appraisal** Only two of the universities surveyed have formal teacher appraisal or evaluation schemes.

**Recommendation** *All English departments should have a transparent teacher appraisal scheme to guarantee the quality of teaching for all stakeholders – national and institutional as well as the students, the teachers themselves and potential employers.*

**3.5.4.4 Continuing Professional Development** CPD provision in most universities is good, but this is not the case in all universities. Teachers have identified several areas relating to EAP where they have particular training needs[109].

**Recommendation** *All English departments should have a full CPD programme supporting departmental and external teacher development. The programmes should be sensitive to the training needs identified by teachers.*

**3.5.4.5 Teacher status** The status of 'instructor' imposes a glass ceiling on the professional careers of some teachers who wish to undertake research and gain higher qualifications in some universities.

**Recommendation** *There should be no 'glass ceiling' preventing instructors from being promoted to academic faculty if they gain the appropriate skills, experience and qualifications, as happens in many other countries.*

---

[109] For a full listing of the skills needed by a university teacher of English, see BALEAP (2008).

# 4 Departmental context: English language teaching

## 4.0 Introduction

This chapter deals with pedagogic issues rather than systemic or organisational ones. The discussion and findings are largely based on the 49 observations which were carried out during visits to the preparatory schools of the 24 universities during the pilot and fieldwork. The basic facts of these observations are summarised in the following table:

| Total | Teacher | | | | | | | Class | | | | | | | |
|---|---|---|---|---|---|---|---|---|---|---|---|---|---|---|---|
| | Gender[110] | | Native/non-native | | Language level | | | Language level | | | Curriculum | | | Size | | |
| | M | F | NS | NNS | B2 | C1/C2 | A1/A2 | B1 | B2 | EGP | EGAP | ESAP | <14 | 15-20 | 21> |
| 49 | 6 | 43 | 9 | 40 | 4 | 45 | 19 | 25 | 5 | 36 | 11 | 2 | 21 | 20 | 8 |

Key:  M = male  NS = native speaker  EGP = English for General Purposes
      F = female  NNS = non-native speaker  EGAP = English for General Academic Purposes
      ESAP = English for Specific Academic Purposes

Figure 33: Summary of Preparatory ELT class observations

From these observations, as well as the teachers' focus groups and questionnaire responses, a number of pedagogic issues have been identified which will be discussed in this chapter:

1 Teachers' English proficiency
2 Use of mother tongue
3 Teachers' qualifications and training
4 Curriculum
5 Teaching materials
6 Textbook dependence
7 Classroom interaction
8 Classroom conditions and resources
9 Use of technology

## 4.1 Teachers' English proficiency

English teachers generally have a good level of English proficiency: 92 per cent were judged to be at CEFR C1/C2 levels and only eight per cent at B2. This is not quite as optimistic as the estimates given by the teachers themselves[111]:

---

[110] Males are somewhat under-represented in the observations – 12 per cent against 25–30 per cent in the questionnaire population
[111] The discrepancy may be because of residual pronunciation errors typical of Turkish speakers; see Thompson 1987

| (N=350) | EMI | T-EMI | TMI | average |
|---|---|---|---|---|
| Bilingual (C2) | 28.9% | 22.8% | 12.0% | 24.6% |
| Advanced (C1) | 68.1% | 75.2% | 88.0% | 73.1% |
| Upper intermediate (B2) | 3.0% | 2.1% | 0.0% | 2.3% |

Figure 34: Teachers' self-assessment of English language proficiency

These figures are good by European and international standards, and confirm that English teachers in Turkey have good standards of English proficiency and are linguistically well-equipped to do their jobs. In addition to their linguistic abilities, most teachers work hard to generate intrinsic motivation in their classes.

## 4.2 Use of mother tongue

It used to be thought that all language lessons should be conducted entirely in the target language, but in recent years it has been widely accepted that the mother tongue (MT) can be used to a limited extent to facilitate understanding and improve the efficiency of classroom management[112]. In the lessons observed during the fieldwork for this project, teachers conducted nearly all lessons in English:

| Use of MT | Number/Percentage of observed lessons |
|---|---|
| Mostly English | 39 (80%) |
| MT used only for clarification | 7 (14%) |
| Much use of mother tongue | 3 (6%) |

Figure 35: Use of Mother Tongue in observed lessons (N=49)

Only three (six per cent) of the observed lessons used the MT excessively, to the point at which the observer (who did not speak Turkish) could not follow the lesson. In fact, one might have expected more use of the MT for greater lesson efficiency. A matter of greater concern was the number of observed lessons where students consistently used the MT, even in student-teacher interaction, without any intervention by the teacher to encourage the use of the target language.

## 4.3 Teachers' qualifications and training

English teachers seem to be well-qualified, with around two-thirds having master's degrees:

---

[112] See Harbord (1992) for a discussion and useful checklist of strategies employing the MT in the ELT classroom.

| (N=350) | EMI | T-EMI | TMI | average |
|---|---|---|---|---|
| PhD | 5.8% | 7.9% | 10.7% | 7.2% |
| Master's degree | 55.8% | 52.7% | 32.1% | 52.4% |
| Bachelor degree | 44.2% | 44.8% | 67.9% | 46.4% |
| Teaching certificate/diploma | 48.7% | 32.7% | 28.6% | 39.5% |

Figure 36: Teachers' qualifications

It would also seem that these qualifications are in subject areas directly related to their profession as English language teachers:

| (N=350) | EMI | T-EMI | TMI | average |
|---|---|---|---|---|
| English language teaching | 61.5% | 63.6% | 57.1% | 62.2% |
| English language & literature | 21.8% | 27.3% | 28.6% | 24.9% |
| Linguistics | 7.7% | 6.7% | 10.7% | 7.4% |
| Education | 12.8% | 7.9% | 7.1% | 10.0% |
| Other [113] | 11.5% | 8.5% | 3.6% | 9.5% |
| Foreign languages | 1.9% | 1.2% | 3.6% | 1.7% |

Figure 37: Subjects of teachers' highest qualifications

However, these qualifications seem to have included little EAP/ESP: Figure 32 revealed that most of the training needs identified by teachers relate to EAP/ESP and further skills in areas such as needs analysis and course design, materials selection and development, and genre analysis would be needed if the curriculum were to be shifted away from the current focus on EGP towards EAP (see Section 4.4 below).

## 4.4 Curriculum

The curriculum used in the classes observed was heavily weighted towards general English – 36 lessons (73 per cent) were EGP, 11 lessons (22 per cent) were EGAP and only 2 (4per cent) ESAP. It has already been argued (Section 3.1.2 above) that a curriculum more relevant to students' needs and academic fields would be likely to improve motivation and make them better equipped with the necessary linguistic and critical thinking skills required for undergraduate studies. In focus group discussions with teachers, several objections were raised to shifting the curriculum emphasis from EGP towards EAP:

- Teachers' lack of training in EAP/ESP (confirmed by Figure 32). This may be true but it really is not an adequate reason for not teaching courses more relevant to students' needs. There are lots of materials and courses available for teachers of EAP and these could and should be made available to preparatory teachers as part of their CPD.

---
[113] American Culture and Literature, Distance Education, Management in Education, Turkish, Cultural Studies, etc.

- EAP is not suitable for elementary learners and there are no suitable materials. While an argument could be made that elementary teachers need a grounding in general English, most preparatory school students have already been exposed to this in high schools, often several times, and they are more likely to be motivated by a fresh approach. Most of the major international ELT publishers now offer low-level EAP materials for elementary learners.
- EGAP materials are too general for students, especially in classes composed of mixed-major students. There seems to be no administrative reason why students could not be grouped by their major, and this was certainly observed in one university where engineers and architects were taught in separate classes (the only two ESAP classes observed). And even if this is not possible, there are techniques for 'personalising' activities and making them more relevant to a student's major. For example, in most academic writing classes, students were shown how to structure an academic essay and were then asked to apply this structure to a topic of interest to all of them (e.g. 'global warming'). A better approach more consistent with international practice would be to ask each student to write an academic essay relevant to his/her subject major (e.g. 'describe one way in which your academic discipline could contribute to solving some of the problems of global warming'). A good example of this was observed in an EGAP speaking class, where students were asked to use the internet to prepare a three-minute group presentation on a hero from their academic field or profession. In reading classes, students can be asked to find their own texts to present to the class, which not only makes the texts more relevant but increases the degree of student independence or autonomy[114].

## 4.5 Teaching materials

In the fieldwork questionnaire, teachers showed that they devote the greatest percentage of their class time to using a coursebook and workbook:

| (N=350) | EMI | T-EMI | TMI | average |
|---|---|---|---|---|
| Coursebook and workbook | 40.6% | 39.5% | 43.5% | 40.6% |
| PC/internet | 28.5% | 26.5% | 27.5% | 27.5% |
| Audio CD/cassette | 24.5% | 24.5% | 22.5% | 24.5% |
| PowerPoint | 23.5% | 21.5% | 23.5% | 22.5% |
| Video/DVD | 20.5% | 23.5% | 22.5% | 21.5% |
| Smartboard | 10.7% | 19.5% | 28.5% | 16.5% |

Figure 38: Percentage of time using resources

A further question confirmed the high use of coursebooks and identified the main source as international published materials, mostly from the UK and, to a lesser extent, the US:

---

[114] See Scott *et al* 1984 for this approach used in a British Council ESP project in Brazilian universities

| (N=350) | EMI | T-EMI | TMI | average |
|---|---|---|---|---|
| International published material | 3.2 | 3.2 | 3.3 | 3.2 |
| My own materials | 2.8 | 2.5 | 2.3 | 2.6 |
| Internet materials | 2.5 | 2.6 | 2.5 | 2.6 |
| Institutional material | 2.7 | 2.3 | 2.2 | 2.4 |
| Locally-published materials | 1.4 | 1.3 | 0.8 | 1.3 |

Figure 39: Proportions of teaching materials used
(Responses on a 0 (= never) – 4 (= every day) scale)

Most of these materials consist not only of a students' textbook, but also a detailed teacher's book and accompanying audio-visual materials, notably 'iTools' for use as an interactive whiteboard. The universal use of these materials confirms that English departments in Turkish universities are well equipped with the latest materials.[115] These are supplemented by 'institutional materials', which are usually in-house materials prepared by a curriculum/materials unit to a high standard to provide additional material and guidance. These suggest a high level of professionalism in English departments, although, as shown in Figure 32, EAP/ESP materials development is the second-ranked training need of English teachers (see 4.4. above).

## 4.6 Textbook dependence

There is, however, a danger of becoming over-dependent on modern materials which are produced to such high standards and come with technological support, and there was some evidence of this in the observed lessons, where over 70 per cent followed the textbook with no or only limited adaptation or use of other resources:

| (N=49) | Number/Percentage of observed lessons |
|---|---|
| Following textbook | 21 (43%) |
| Some adaptation of textbook | 14 (28.5%) |
| Using a range of resources | 14 (28.5%) |

Figure 40: Materials used in observed lessons

This situation was confirmed by the degree of planning evident in the lessons observed, where nearly 80 per cent were judged to have been planned using simply the textbook and its supporting resources:

---

[115] However, there is some concern over the widespread use of pirated students' books in some universities.

| (N=49) | Number/Percentage of observed lessons |
|---|---|
| Going beyond textbook | 11 (22%) |
| Following textbook | 38 (78%) |
| Little evident planning | 0 (0%) |

Figure 41: Evidence of planning in observed lessons

Given the quality of the materials available and the heavy teaching load of most teachers, it is to be expected that most lessons would be planned around the textbook, but the lack of any adaptation causes concern for several reasons: it limits the amount of variety in the lesson; it limits the amount of personalisation to the students' context and interests; it limits any adaptation of tasks to students' fields of academic study (see 4.4 above); it limits opportunities for classroom interaction (see 4.7 below); it limits opportunities to use technology (see 4.9 below); and it restricts the personal initiative of teachers. In some cases it seemed that the strict following of the textbook was a departmental requirement, especially where the curriculum unit had prepared additional materials that sequenced lessons in great detail, but in focus groups teachers frequently mentioned that they felt happiest when the departments granted them a certain amount of freedom to adapt the materials or introduce their own materials into lessons. Despite the high average for using own materials in Figure 39, little evidence of this was seen in the lessons observed.

## 4.7 Classroom interaction

The main limitation of the lessons observed – both EGP and EGAP – was the lack of opportunities for students to speak. In the 49 lessons observed, only seven (14 per cent) were noted as having anything more than limited student talking time through pair or group work, while 16 (33 per cent) were described as 'teacher-dominated', with teacher talking time (either teacher monologue or teacher-student interaction) significantly greater than student talking time:

| (N=49) | Number/Percentage of observed lessons |
|---|---|
| A lot of student talking time | 7 (14%) |
| Limited student talking time | 26 (53%) |
| Teacher-dominated interaction | 16 (33%) |

Figure 42: Interaction in observed lessons

The lack of student talking time has several serious implications:

- Students have little opportunity to practise their speaking skills if the dominant interaction pattern is teacher-student rather than student-student. Speaking skills are considered especially important by students as skills in their own right as well as the main indicator of their language proficiency. Classroom observations revealed that Turkish students are weak at speaking by comparison with other skills, especially reading.

- Poor speaking impacts on students' academic performance in their undergraduate programmes, especially their ability to contribute to class discussion:

  > Due to the lack of speaking practice we are now experiencing difficulty in understanding lectures. We do not have enough confidence to speak in lectures. Participating in the lectures is a real problem for us.[116]

- Lack of interaction in classes encourages students to be passive in class, both in their preparatory-year language classes and, later, in their undergraduate programmes.

- Restricting students' opportunities to contribute actively to classes tends to make lessons uninteresting, reducing intrinsic motivation.

The lack of interaction was evident in several ways: teachers consistently preferred to elicit answers from individual students rather than have students discuss answers in pairs or groups; group activities in the textbook were often missed out; there were very few additional speaking activities added to the textbook exercises; opportunities to integrate speaking with writing (e.g. through group writing tasks), listening (e.g. through getting students to share and compare answers), reading (e.g. jigsaw reading where each student has a part of a text and they have to construct the complete text in groups), grammar (e.g. paired dictation) or with a range of skills (e.g. projects) were nearly always missed. A whole range of speaking techniques have been developed in the past 25 years – information gap activities, pyramid discussions, information transfer, role play, simulation, informal debates, etc. – but these were included only once or twice in all of the 49 lessons observed. In the few cases where these techniques were used the results were dramatic: classes were dynamic and the degree of intrinsic motivation increased. In most of these cases, the teachers involved had taken CELTA or DELTA qualifications, or, in one case, the teacher was a CELTA tutor. Teachers in these lessons also seemed able to incorporate simple technological techniques (see 4.9 below).

## 4.8 Classroom conditions and resources

As can be seen from Figure 33, the majority of classes were 'small' (14 or fewer) or 'medium' (15-20). Very few were 'large' (21 or more) and the average size was much smaller than most undergraduate classes observed (see Chapter 5). This situation was largely confirmed by the teachers' questionnaire (average 20) and the students' questionnaire, although both students and teachers cited large classes as one of the major reasons impeding students' language progress (see Figure 25). The students were also asked how many students they would like in their classes and the result was a preference for even smaller classes:

---
[116] Kırkgöz 2009: 88

| (N=4320) | EMI | T-EMI | TMI | average |
|---|---|---|---|---|
| How many students are there in your English language classes? | 19.5 | 21.8 | 20.0 | 20.6 |
| How many students would you like in your English language classes? | 14.0 | 14.3 | 13.7 | 14.1 |

Figure 43: Class size[117]

However, class size must be seen as not merely a matter of the staff-student ratio but also the number of students in a classroom of a given size. Only in one state university was the class size so large that the arrangement was uncomfortable and the teacher unable to circulate to see how students were managing with the tasks.

Most classrooms were well-furnished, well-lit, well-ventilated and all were equipped with whiteboards. Every classroom was equipped with a projector or beamer to which a computer could be linked. In almost every lesson, the teacher had a computer available, but in most cases they used their own rather than an institutional one. In most cases, the IWB or iTools materials were projected on to a traditional whiteboard but in some cases the room was equipped with a Smartboard. In many cases, classrooms were not linked to the internet or had poor connections. The level of technology was in all cases adequate, but the sound quality was often poor as it relied on the speakers in the teacher's laptop computer.

## 4.9 Use of technology

Although all classrooms were equipped with adequate levels of technology, the use of this technology was somewhat ineffective[118]:

| Use of technology | Number/Percentage of observed lessons |
|---|---|
| Good/original | 10 (20%) |
| Following publishers' IWB materials | 36 (73%) |
| None | 7 (14%) |

Figure 44: Use of technology (N=49)
(Figures total more than 100 per cent because some teachers followed the publishers' IWB materials and also made use of additional materials)

In some cases (20 per cent), the use of technology was imaginative and effective: in particular, teachers (some of whom said that they were not particularly computer-literate) used the internet or, especially, got their students to use their mobile phones in lessons. Two good examples were seen of students using their mobile phones for group writing tasks, which they then sent to the teacher by email, and the teacher then projected the paragraphs on to the whiteboard. In other examples, students worked in pairs or teams to do quizzes

---
[117] See Çetinsaya 2014; 129 for more general statistics on staff: student ratios in Turkish universities.
[118] Using ITC/computers in the classroom was ranked 2= among teachers' training needs (see Figure 32).

or games using Kahoot[119], which proved very motivating and also helped to generate student-student interaction in the classroom.

In most cases (73 per cent), however, teachers seemed content or perhaps even compelled to use the interactive whiteboard (IWB) materials supplied by the publishers with the textbooks used by the class. This is another instance of over-dependence on textbooks (See 4.6 above).

There were several cases where technology was not used at all but this did not necessarily lead to a poor lesson; indeed, one of the best lessons observed involved no technology at all. In all cases the technology was available, but in some cases the teacher chose not to use it because it was not appropriate or necessary, for example when students were giving poster presentations.

## 4.10 Findings and recommendations

The findings of Section 4 are summarised in the following paragraphs and the implications for English language teaching are made clear. Recommendations based on these findings then follow.

**4.10.1 Teachers' English proficiency** The English proficiency level of the overwhelming majority is very good, but there seems to be no established CEFR standard in all skills for university teachers, as in many countries.

**Recommendation** *CoHE and all universities should set a minimum standard of C1 for all university English teachers, preferably with evidence from an international examination that assesses all four skills.*

**4.10.2 Use of mother tongue** There is very little use of Turkish in most classes. There are times when explanations and instructions can be given more efficiently in the mother tongue, especially with elementary students.

**Recommendation** *Guidelines should be drawn up for the appropriate and limited use of the mother tongue in English lessons.*

**4.10.3 Teachers' qualifications and training** English teachers are generally well qualified, with many having higher degrees. Nevertheless, the teachers themselves identified further training priorities, especially in the area of EAP/ ESP, and further training needs emerge from this baseline study.

**Recommendation** *Institutional and national training programmes should be implemented to meet the training needs of university English teachers. Courses in various aspects of EAP/ESP course design and evaluation should be one area of priority.*

**4.10.4 Curriculum** The curriculum in the majority of preparatory classes is

---

[119] A game-based computer system which allows teachers to download, adapt or create quizzes for the class. See https://getkahoot.com

mostly EGP, with some EGAP in the second semester or with more advanced students. The undergraduate curriculum is mostly EGAP. Few universities have developed needs-based undergraduate programmes customised to students' academic disciplines and interests.

**Recommendation** *Universities should acquire and apply skills in needs analysis in order to develop EAP/ESP programmes that are more relevant to the general and specific academic needs of preparatory and graduate programmes.*

**4.10.5 Materials** Modern, international materials with good computer software are available in all universities.

**Recommendation** *Universities should continue to be supplied with modern, international teaching materials selected for relevance and effectiveness.*

**4.10.6 Textbook dependence** There is evidence of textbook dependence in many universities, with most teachers planning their lessons around the set coursebook and with few attempts to go beyond the textbook to develop more interactive or subject-relevant activities.

**Recommendation** *Training courses should be established to reduce teachers' dependency on textbooks and to explore ways of adapting textbooks to the personal and disciplinary interests of students.*

**4.10.7 Classroom interaction** The main problem in most English classes is the lack of student-student interaction, restricting students' opportunities to develop their speaking skills. This has short-term consequences for student motivation and a longer-term impact on students' abilities to take part actively in class discussions in their undergraduate programmes.

**Recommendation** *Training courses should be devised to address the number one shortcoming of university English teaching: the lack of student-student interaction in the language classroom. The courses should focus on integrating speaking into all activities, including activities practising reading, writing, listening and grammar.*

**4.10.8 Classroom conditions and resources** Most classrooms are sufficiently large and well-equipped, but these standards are not met in one or two cases. Most classrooms have adequate technical resources, although teachers often have to supply their own computers, there is limited internet access and there are often problems with acoustics because of the shortcomings of laptop speaker systems.

**Recommendation** *Standards should be established for the numbers of students to be accommodated in every classroom. Internet access, sound systems and* *computer provision should be improved.*

**4.10.9 Use of technology** Teachers are largely dependent on the IWB materials supplied by the publishers of their textbooks. While this situation generally leads to adequate lessons, it limits the intrinsic motivation of the students and the creativity and freedom of the teachers. In the very good lessons observed, teachers always departed from the standard software provided by publishers.

**Recommendation** *Training courses should be developed in the use of technology in the ELT classroom, focusing on tech equipment such as the use of students' mobile phones.*

# 5 Department context: English as medium of instruction

## 5.0 Introduction

The broader contextual and policy issues relating to EMI have already been discussed in Chapter 2. This chapter deals with issues relating to academic or departmental lessons/lectures delivered through the medium of English. The discussion and findings are largely based on questionnaires given to academic faculty and the 16 observations which were carried out during visits to academic departments of the 24 universities during the pilot and fieldwork. The basic facts of these observations are summarised in the following table:

| Total | Academic faculty number | | | | | | | | | | Class | | | | | | |
|---|---|---|---|---|---|---|---|---|---|---|---|---|---|---|---|---|---|
| (N=16) | Gender | | Native/Non-native | | Language level | | | Academic discipline | | | | Approach | | | Class size | | |
| | M | F | NS | NNS | B1 | B2 | C1/C2 | Sci/Eng | Soc Sci | Law | ESP | CLIL | EMI | <14 | 15-20 | 21> |
| 16 | 8 | 8 | 3 | 13 | 1 | 4 | 11 | 6 | 9 | 1 | 4 | 1 | 11 | 3 | 3 | 10 |

Key  M = male          NS = native speaker          Sci = sciences          ESP = English for Specific Purposes
     F = female        NNS = non-native speaker     Eng = engineering      CLIL = Content & language integrated learning
                                                    Soc = social           EMI = English as medium of instruction

Figure 45: Summary of departmental EMI lessons

A number of pedagogic issues have been identified which will be discussed in this chapter:

1  Approaches to English-mediated education
2  Issues in English-mediated education

## 5.1 Approaches to English-mediated education

English-mediated education in Turkish universities embraces a spectrum of approaches to the teaching of academic content through English. Three main approaches may usefully be distinguished[120]:

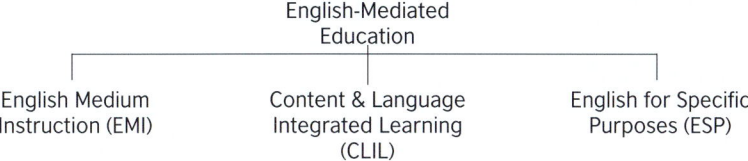

Figure 46: Approaches to English-Mediated Education in Turkish Universities

---

[120] A fourth approach is English as a lingua franca in academic settings (ELFA – see Maurenen et al. 2010) but this was not observed in Turkish universities.

Each of these terms needs definition and clarification so that the three can be clearly distinguished:

- **English as Medium of Instruction (EMI)** EMI may be defined as:

    The use of the English language to teach academic subjects in countries or jurisdictions where the first language (L1) of the majority of the population is not English.[121]

    The aim of EMI is to teach content (economics, physics, etc.) through English. This definition makes it clear that English is being used merely to 'carry' the academic content. It is usually assumed that the academic teacher is responsible for transmitting this content, but takes little or no responsibility for explaining the language (apart from specialist terminology). In this way, the academic may often seem to deliver a lesson or lecture as if s/he were working in an L1 context. Very often, the academic may have received his/her graduate training in an L1 context and so tends to teach as s/he was taught.

- **Content and Language Integrated Learning (CLIL)** As the term CLIL makes plain, in this approach the teacher or lecturer assumes responsibility for both content and language, and in this way it is distinguished from EMI:

    Whereas CLIL has a clear objective of furthering both content and language as declared in its title, EMI does not (necessarily) have that objective.[122]

    The aim of CLIL is to teach both content and language. The teacher (usually an academic rather than a language teacher) assumes responsibility for both the content and the language, and employs various strategies to assist students' understanding and to check that they have understood. The academic will normally have had some level of CLIL training. In recent years CLIL has become the dominant approach to English-mediated education in many European countries, especially those where international degree programmes are offered.[123]

- **English for Specific Purposes (ESP)** The aim of ESP is to teach the specialist language[124] rather than the content. ESP is usually taught by a language teacher rather than an academic and is defined in terms of purpose or need:

    ESP (English for Specific Purposes) involves teaching and learning the specific skills and language needed by particular learners for a particular purpose.[125]

    The purpose may be academic (EAP) or occupational (EOP) and the focus may be narrow or specific (ESAP/ESOP) or broad or general (EGAP/EGOP). In ESP the focus is always on the language and the content is merely the 'carrier' which is used for purposes of illustration, relevance and motivation.

---

[121] Dearden 2014: 2
[122] Dearden 2014: 4
[123] For a recent overview of CLIL in higher education, see Ruiz-Garrido & Campoy-Cubillo (eds) (2013). For a survey from a Turkish perspective, see Darn (n/d)
[124] This involves all aspects of language (grammar, language functions, discourse features, generic structure, vocabulary, etc), not just specialist terminology.
[125] Day & Krzanowski 2011: 5

In Turkish universities one may encounter all three approaches: ESP is normally taught as language support and is usually not credit-bearing; CLIL is rare and only one example was observed during the fieldwork; EMI is common in those universities where English is designated as the medium of instruction for some or all of the programmes, but in practice EMI may involve a range of teaching strategies and varying proportions of English and Turkish.

## 5.2 Issues in EMI

The issues discussed in this section arise from the observations carried out during the fieldwork and the questionnaires completed by 64 EMI faculty members in 19 universities. The principal issues are: introducing EMI, language proficiency, responsibility for learning, teaching strategies employed, and training for EMI.

**5.2.1 Introducing EMI** Decisions on language of instruction in Turkish universities are delegated to the institution, but it is not always clear at what level the actual decision is made – institutional or departmental. Faculty surveyed in this project gave mixed answers to the question, 'Who decides what courses are taught in English?"

| (N=64) | EMI | T-EMI | average |
|---|---|---|---|
| The university | 69,8% | 34,8% | 58,2% |
| Department/Head of Department | 16,3% | 47,8% | 26,9% |
| Individual academic teacher | 4,7% | 4,3% | 4,5% |
| The Ministry/YÖK | 2,3% | 0% | 1.5% |
| The students | 2,3% | 0% | 1.5% |
| Other/No answer | 4,6% | 13,9% | 7,4% |

Figure 47: Decisions on introducing EMI

These results suggest that in EMI universities decisions on language of instruction are mostly institutional, whereas in TMI universities greater initiative lies with departments.

Universities were asked if English language proficiency is a factor in staff recruitment (N=21). Four responded that it was not, citing CoHE regulations, whereas 17 stated that it was. In all of these cases universities demanded certificates of an accredited English language examination, usually an international one. Six universities explained that they also ask for a demonstration lesson/lecture to be given in English at the time of interview. Nevertheless, universities often stated that the major restriction on EMI and T-EMI programmes is the lack of academic staff with sufficient levels of English proficiency to teach such programmes.

When asked if incentives were given to academics who teach in English, the majority answered that there were none. This contrasts with some other countries, where salary bonuses or conference support may be given.

**5.2.2 English language proficiency** Faculty teaching through English generally rate their English proficiency as high:

| (N=64) | EMI | T-EMI | Average |
|---|---|---|---|
| Bilingual (C2) | 2.7% | 9.1% | 5.1% |
| Advanced (C1) | 89.2% | 77.3% | 84.7% |
| Intermediate (B1-B2) | 8.1% | 13.6% | 10.2% |

Figure 48: EMI faculty English proficiency levels

These self-assessments broadly correspondent to the observer's evaluations, where 69 per cent were judged to be CEFR level C1-C2 and 25 per cent CEFR level B2. CEFR level B2 is usually regarded as the minimum for teaching through EMI and, by this standard, the majority of faculty meet international norms. For the minority who need further language improvement and for those who aspire to teaching through EMI but do not have the necessary standard of proficiency, there are now special coursebooks for academics available.

**5.2.3 Responsibility for learning** In line with the definition of EMI offered above, EMI faculty members stated that they offered little or limited language support to their students:

| (N=64) | EMI | T-EMI | average |
|---|---|---|---|
| Translating specialist terms into Turkish | 58.3% | 58.3% | 58.3% |
| Translating difficult sections of lectures into Turkish | 52.8% | 50.0% | 51.7% |
| None/almost none | 21.6% | 25.0% | 23.0% |
| Providing bilingual glossaries | 2.8% | 16.7% | 8.3% |
| Other | 0.5% | 4.25% | 1.7% |

Figure 49: English language support given by EMI faculty

Several points emerge from these results: faculty clearly take little responsibility for language support for their students; support, when it is given, is largely a matter of vocabulary, and mostly employs translation; and faculty make it plain that they have no other language-support strategies. All of these points are consistent with an EMI approach rather than a CLIL or ESP approach. The crucial difference is the language level at which the lesson or lecture is delivered:

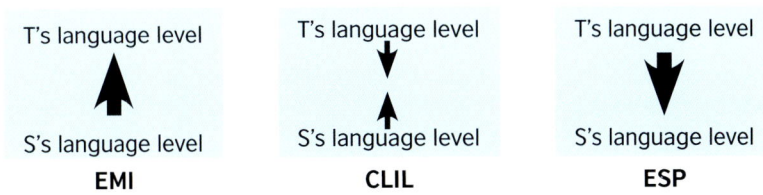

Figure 50: Language 'accommodation'

Figure 50 illustrates the level of language adjustment or 'accommodation' in the three situations:

- **EMI** The academic teacher (T) delivers the lesson/lecture at his/her own language level, which is usually several levels above that of the students (S), and makes little or no effort to adjust his/her own English down to a level closer to that of the students[126]. The teacher sees the language difference as the students' problem and provides little or no support.
- **ESP** The language teacher (T) brings his/her language level down to that of the students or to a level slightly above (L+1). The teacher sees the language difference as his/her responsibility and provides as much support as possible to raise the students' level.
- **CLIL** The academic teacher (T) recognises the students' language problems and tries to modify his/her own language so that it is closer to the students' level, and also adopts a range of strategies to try to facilitate communication and comprehension. In the one CLIL lesson that was observed during the fieldwork, it was notable that the lecturer used not only a broader range of strategies, but used them in ways which integrated the content and the language, for example by drawing attention to language points in the text that was being discussed in the lecture.

**5.2.4 EMI teaching strategies** Most EMI teachers admitted, when interviewed, that they were unaware of the strategies they used to try to ensure that their students' understood their lessons. It is therefore informative to compare the strategies that they mentioned in Figure 49 with the actual strategies used in the EMI lessons that were observed. Six groups of strategies were identified during the observations:

- **Mother tongue strategies** These are strategies where the academic uses Turkish in various ways to try to ensure comprehension. Mother tongue (MT) strategies were the ones that were mentioned most by the academics in the questionnaire (see Figure 49 above) but were in fact rarely used during the observed lessons:

---

[126] See also van den Berg & Ross 1999 for a rather similar analysis.

| Strategy | Occurrences during observed lessons |
|---|---|
| Lesson mostly in MT | 1 |
| MT used for summaries | 1 |
| MT used for clarification | 2 |
| Answers questions in MT | 0 |
| MT used for technical terms | 0 |

Figure 51: Mother-tongue strategies used by EMI teachers (N=16)

This lack of MT strategies had not been anticipated, especially as these had been the strategies that EMI academics stated that they used most frequently. However, it may have been that there was an observer paradox: the observer's presence modified the academics' behaviour and they consciously or unconsciously suppressed strategies that they normally used. These strategies can be very effective for students speaking the same MT as that of the academic, but they can be extremely frustrating for international students who do not speak Turkish.

- **English language strategies** These are strategies used by academics who are generally comfortable or confident using English, and in fact they were used quite frequently in the observed lessons:

| Strategy | Occurrences during observed lessons |
|---|---|
| Lesson mostly in English | 15 |
| Answers questions in English | 7 |
| Modifies English for audience | 4 |

Figure 52: English language strategies used by EMI teachers (N=16)

The main strategy was that English was used almost entirely in every observed lesson except one, but again the observer paradox may be at work. The most notable finding is that in only 25 per cent of the cases was there evidence that the academic was modifying his/her language in a way that is sometimes called 'teacherese' (the language used by teachers to their students with features including simplified vocabulary, slower delivery, clearer pronounciation, higher levels of complete sentences and grammatical accuracy, reduction in shortened forms).

- **Repair strategies** As the name suggests, these are strategies used by the academic when s/he perceives that there is a problem. Experienced EMI teachers will use anticipatory repair strategies, i.e. knowing that there may be problems, the teacher tries to check whether the class has understood rather than wait for students to ask questions or look blank. Repair strategies were used quite frequently in the observed lessons:

| Strategy | Occurrences during observed lessons |
|---|---|
| Invites questions/comprehension checks | 15 |
| Permits interruptions for questions | 3 |
| Uses comprehension questions | 13 |

Figure 53: Repair strategies used by EMI teachers (N=16)

Comprehension checks of both kinds were used widely, but specific comprehension questions are generally more effective than more open "Any questions?", "Do you understand?" questions. In both cases, however, it was notable that there were no responses from students. A silent response to a specific comprehension question could be further evidence of students' unwillingness to participate actively in lessons (see 4.7 above), but, more importantly in this context, it means that the academic is not using the strategy to gauge comprehension.

- **Lesson structuring** Clear structuring is an obvious way of helping students follow the lesson. These were used in approximately half of the observed lessons:

| Strategy | Occurrences during observed lessons |
|---|---|
| T announces aims/lesson structure | 8 |
| T uses key questions to structure lesson | 9 |
| T uses PowerPoint to structure lesson | 7 |

Figure 54: Lesson-structuring strategies used by EMI teachers (N=16)

These are strategies which are not specific to EMI lessons and should be features of any good lesson/lecture, and so the fact that they were not more widely used is cause for concern as it suggests that TMI lessons are equally unstructured.

- **Visual-aid support** In classes where students have problems with English, especially spoken English, a useful group of strategies involves using visual-aids. Several of these strategies again involve the use of PowerPoint:

| Strategy | Occurrences during observed lessons |
|---|---|
| Ss have PowerPoint slides as handouts | 1 |
| Ss have PowerPoint slides online | 2 |
| T uses whiteboard extensively | 6 |

Figure 55: Visual-aid strategies used by EMI teachers (N=16)

It was also notable that in only one case did the students seem to have access to the PowerPoint slides as handouts and networked to their computers. In most high-ranking European universities it is now a requirement that PowerPoint slides are available to students, usually via the university intranet[127].

- **Textual support** The final group of strategies involves supplying students with parallel content to the lecture in written form. Again, there was rather limited use of these strategies:

| Strategy | Occurrences during observed lessons |
|---|---|
| Ss referred to textbooks, articles, etc | 5 |
| Use of equations, examples, tasks, etc | 8 |
| T gives handouts | 3 |

Figure 56: Textual support strategies used by EMI teachers (N=16)

These are strategies that could be expected in any TMI lecture, raising again the broader issue of the quality of university teaching and the need for training.

**5.2.5 Training for EMI** The need for language proficiency improvement has already been mentioned (see 5.2.2 above), but there would seem to be a need for broader training in techniques which would improve standards of teaching and learning in EMI lectures. As has already been said, the EMI academics stated that they were unaware of the strategies that they used, and were also unaware of strategies that might be effective:

> Even if staff have an adequate command of English (and questions often remain over verification and appropriate staff development opportunities), they are unlikely to have specialist knowledge of the particular demands of university-level education through an L2, where mixed ability becomes the norm and complex content exacerbates already high cognitive processing loads.[128]

Academics seemed aware that there was a need for training in EMI teaching but indicated that professional development was rather limited[129]:

---
[127] For a fuller discussion of the advantages and limitations of PowerPoint, see Brazeau (2006)
[128] Marsh and Laitinen 2005, quoted by Coleman 2006: 7
[129] See also Başıbek et al 2013: 1824 for recommendations for training in the improvement of lecturing skills in EMI.

| Is training to help you teaching in English available in your university? | EMI | T-EMI | average |
|---|---|---|---|
| Yes | 35.9% | 40.0% | 37.5% |
| No | 59.0% | 56.0% | 57.8% |
| No response | 5.1% | 4.0% | 4.7% |

Figure 57: Availability of EMI training (N=64)

It also seems that this is part of a wider problem – that CPD is not widely or regularly available to academics in universities in Turkey:

| How often is this training available? | EMI | T-EMI | average |
|---|---|---|---|
| More than once a year | 9.1% | 30.0% | 19.0% |
| Once a year | 27.3% | 0% | 14.3% |
| Occasionally/sometimes | 36.4% | 60.0% | 47.6% |
| Other | 27.3% | 10.0% | 19.0% |

Figure 58: Frequency of CPD for EMI academics (N-64)

This situation – especially in TMI universities where an element of EMI has been introduced – is of serious concern as it undermines the issues of quality and quality assurance across all EMI programmes.

EMI training is now an established practice in other European countries and it might be of interest to outline the communication issues that such a training course might focus on. Klaassen and de Graaff (2001) list five possible issues and then show how these were used to develop an EMI training course for engineering lecturers in the Netherlands:

| Training aspects | | Training objectives |
|---|---|---|
| Effective lecturing behaviour which suffers from a switch in language | → | Knowing which strong and weak points I have when having to give EMI lectures. |
| Effective lecturing behaviour which addresses the needs of non-native speaking students | → | Knowing which effective lecturing behaviour can be used to support students understanding of the lecture |
| Awareness of second language acquisition difficulties | → | Being able to recognize the problems my students have with EMI. |
| Reflection on beliefs and actual lecturing behaviour | | |
| Cultural issues if relevant to the first four aspects | | |

Figure 59: EMI Training (Klaassen and de Graaff 2001)

## 5.3 Findings and recommendations

The findings of Section 5 are summarised in the following paragraphs and the implications for English language teaching are made clear. Recommendations based on these findings then follow.

**5.3.1 Approaches to English-mediated education** English-mediated education is widespread in Turkish universities (see Section 2) but the approach adopted is mainly EMI. While there are historical reasons for this approach, there are other models which have been developed more recently, in particular CLIL, which is now used increasingly by high-ranking universities in other European countries but which is largely unknown in Turkey.

**Recommendation** *English-mediated education should move from the EMI approach towards Content and Language Integrated Learning (CLIL).*

**5.3.2 Issues in EMI** The issues surrounding EMI seem to be unknown to both the institutions and the individual academics teaching through EMI.

**5.3.2.1 Introducing EMI** The medium of instruction is largely an institutional decision, but most universities take English proficiency into consideration when recruiting staff. In most cases, however, the criterion is merely performance in an accredited English language examination and the recruitment of sufficient staff with adequate levels of English to teach EMI programmes remains a problem.

**Recommendation** *In order to ensure that all academic staff can both teach in English and carry out their research using English-language resources, recruitment should take full account of English proficiency and teaching skills.*

**5.3.2.2 English language proficiency** English proficiency levels of EMI academics are mostly good. In a few cases, English levels were judged to be inadequate and it is not clear if or how the language needs of academics who do not currently teach through EMI are being addressed.

**Recommendation** *English for Academics (EfA) courses should be offered to all academics to upgrade their English language proficiency.*

**5.3.2.3 Responsibility for learning** In most cases, academics see learning as being the responsibility of the student, and make few attempts to consider the language problems of students, apart from providing some bilingual materials for specialist vocabulary.

**Recommendation** *As part of a CLIL approach to English-mediated education, staff should learn to take responsibility for their students' learning.*

**5.3.2.4 Teaching strategies** Academics are largely unaware of the strategies they use when teaching, both through EMI and (apparently) TMI. Many of the strategies they do use are not used effectively and they do not meet standard practices in universities elsewhere in Europe.

**Recommendation** *As part of a CLIL approach to English-mediated education, academic staff should acquire a broader range of teaching strategies, including the effective use of PowerPoint and other technology.*

**5.3.2.5 Training for EMI** There is very little training available in most universities in effective approaches to EMI teaching. This seems to be part of a wider shortage of CPD provision.

**Recommendation** *All universities should introduce regular CPD programmes. Training courses in EMI/CLIL should be offered to all staff teaching through the medium of English.*

# 6 Summary findings, recommendations and conclusions

## 6.0 Introduction

Detailed findings and recommendations have been given at the ends of Chapters 1-4. In this final chapter summary findings and key recommendations – one for each chapter – will be presented. There are also impact analyses showing the possible results if these recommendations are implemented in full.

## 6.1 Findings and recommendations

### 6.1.1 International context: globalisation

In contrast to other G20 countries, Turkey has focused on quantity in recent years by significantly expanding the number and size of its universities[130]. While there has also been an improvement in quality, with a number of universities performing well in the *Times Higher Education Supplement* global university rankings, there are over 150 universities that fall outside the world's top 1,000 and 100 that fall outside the world's top 2,000 universities, according to Turkey's own URAP rankings. Turkey's 'English deficit' is a major factor affecting the quality of higher education, restricting access to academic resources, international research publication and the mobility of staff and students.

**Recommendation**: *Consideration should be given to creating and funding a project to enhance the quality of universities in Turkey. This would have two major aims:*
a) *To identify and support a tier of high-quality research universities in the top 200 in the global league tables.*
b) *To enhance the quality of teaching, research and resources in the large number of universities that currently fall outside the top 1,000 in the URAP rankings.*

English proficiency levels of students and, in particular, academic staff should form a key part of this project in order to:

- improve access to English-language academic and research resources
- enhance research publication and dissemination
- enhance opportunities for international co-operation in research
- encourage student mobility, in particular by attracting international students to EMI graduate programmes
- encourage staff mobility, including doctoral studies and exchange visits by Turkish academics, and teaching and research attachments by foreign academics.

---

[130] See Çokgezen 2014: 3 for the ways in which this has been achieved.

### 6.1.2 National context: language of instruction

Turkey has a long history of university education in both Turkish and English, and, more recently, mixed-medium Turkish - English instruction. While EMI universities have traditionally been 'more favoured and popular for students and parents in comparison to universities without EMI'[131], there are strong arguments for strengthening the quantity and quality of TMI programmes, in particular because the current English proficiency levels of both academic staff and students restrict effective learning. Mixed-medium T-EMI teaching has, from the evidence in this survey, proved largely ineffective, with staff and students developing strategies for circumventing the use of English in favour of Turkish.

**Recommendation** *It is recommended that the question of languages of instruction in Turkish universities should be* re-examined and re-balanced.

- **Turkish medium** More focus, status and resources should be given to TMI programmes.
  It is suggested that parallel TMI and EMI programmes should be introduced (as already happens in some universities in Turkey) and students should be permitted to access programmes and be assessed in either or both languages. It is calculated that this parallel TMI/EMI model would be more cost effective than the current mixed-medium programmes.

- **English medium** While it is not recommended that current undergraduate EMI programmes should be phased out, it is suggested that new ones should not be introduced until secondary schools produce graduates with intermediate (CEFR B1) levels of English proficiency.
  It is also recommended that the focus of new EMI programmes should be at the graduate rather than the undergraduate level.

- **Mixed medium** No new mixed-medium T-EMI programmes should be authorised and existing T-EMI programmes should be phased out as soon as possible, and replaced by parallel EMI and TMI programmes.

### 6.1.3 Institutional context: language teaching programmes

The current distribution and curriculum of English language teaching in Turkish universities do not give full support to the academic programmes or internationalisation. Students enter preparatory school with low English proficiency levels and low motivation. Preparatory school classes do not fully address these problems as the curriculum is perceived to be lacking in relevance and the classes are not delivered at the time in a student's academic career when they could be most effective.

---

[131] Başıbek *et al* 2013: 1819; see Çokgezen 2014 for factors affecting university choice.

**Recommendation** *Systemic changes should be made in three areas:*

**a) Eligibility and standards:** Preparatory classes should voluntary and normally available only to EMI students. The threshold for entry to preparatory school should be raised to CEFR A2. The exit standards for preparatory schools should be raise to CEFR B2 in all skills for linguistically-demanding programmes and CEFR B1+ for linguistically less-demanding programmes[132]. Exit and entry levels should be assessed through valid examinations assessing all four skills in order to ensure that standards are met and maintained. Students who do not meet these standards should be redirected to TMI programmes or universities.

**b) Curriculum:** The curriculum should be shifted away from English for General Purposes (EGP) towards English for General Academic Purposes (EGAP), and EGAP classes should be customised to cater for students' specialist academic fields. An elective English for Occupational Purposes (EOP) course should be available in the final undergraduate year for those seeking jobs. The curriculum for all of these programmes should be based on a full needs analysis.

**c) Distribution:** Credit-bearing English language courses should be maintained throughout all undergraduate and graduate programmes. These courses should be requirements for all EMI students but elective for TMI students. An elective English for Occupational Purposes (EOP) course should be available in the final undergraduate year for those seeking jobs.

### 6.1.4 Departmental context: English language teaching

The English proficiency levels and qualifications of English teachers in universities are very good, but two widespread shortcomings were observed:

**a)** Most teachers have little or no training in the teaching of EAP/ESP and consequently they lack the skills to develop needs-based EGAP curricula or to customise materials and activities to fit the specialist academic disciplines of students.

**b)** Most teachers constantly miss opportunities to introduce student-student interaction in the classroom. In the short term, this reduces students' progress in speaking skills and in the longer-term it undermines their confidence and ability to participate in class discussion or debate on their academic undergraduate programmes.

**Recommendation** *English teachers should have greater opportunities to access professional development as part of a quality assurance and accreditation scheme. In particular, training should be available in two vital areas:*

**a) EAP/ESP:** All English teachers should undergo a short, intensive training programme in EAP/ESP[133], and some teachers in each university should be offered longer-term training such as that available by distance from some universities[134].

---

[132] See Shatrova 2014: 152: `Some Turkish instructors considered the expectation to bring the students to B2 level "with 700 hours within a year not realistic". They believed that B1 was more doable; therefore the expectations should be lowered.'
[133] Perhaps based on Day and Krzanowski 2011
[134] e.g. the distance MA module offered by the universities of Aston, Bristol, Coventry, Essex, Manchester, Reading and Warwick

**b) Teaching speaking skills**: All teachers should undergo training in techniques for incorporating student-student interaction at every stage of the lesson, with speaking integrated into every activity, regardless of the skill being practised. ELT publishers may offer such training as part of the package of materials sold to a university.

### 6.1.5 Departmental context: English as medium of instruction

The English proficiency levels of EMI academics generally meet international standards, but senior academics in some universities reported problems in finding enough academics with adequate levels of English to meet current requirements or expand EMI programmes. EMI academics do not generally accommodate students' language difficulties and regard EMI learning as the students' responsibility. This approach arises because few academics have been offered any training in EMI teaching and little training of this kind seems to be available in Turkish universities.

**Recommendation** *The approach to English-mediated education should be shifted from EMI to CLIL (Content and Language Integrated Learning) in line with developments in most European countries. EMI academics should be required to undergo training to take more responsibility for their students' learning by adopting a range of language and technological strategies to facilitate learning.*

### 6.2 Impact analysis: university quality

While other emerging G20 countries such as Russia, China, India and South Korea have launched projects to enhance the quality and standing of their universities, Turkey has focused on quantity and instituted a massive expansion of university student numbers. It is recommended that the Turkish government should launch a similar project to improve the quality of universities. This section summarises what could be achieved if these recommendations of this report are implemented in full:

| Step | Action | Recommendation | Impact |
|---|---|---|---|
| 1 | Support for research universities | Create and fund a project to identify and support a tier of high-quality research universities in the top 200 in the global league tables. | This would enable top Turkish universities to maintain and improve their ranking. The project would involve many initiatives (enhanced resources, improved qualifications, travel opportunities, quality assurance, research assessment, etc.), but it would also require improving the English-language proficiency of academic staff. Improved English would facilitate:<br>• international research collaboration |

| Step | Action | Recommendation | Impact |
|---|---|---|---|
| | | | • research publication and dissemination<br>• the development of new postgraduate programmes<br>• attracting more international students from outside the Turkic-/Turkish-speaking region<br>• attracting international staff. |
| 2 | Support for research inactive universities | *Create and fund a project to enhance the quality of teaching, research and resources in the large number of universities that currently fall outside the top 1,000 in the URAP rankings.* | The project would aim to enhance the academic quality and research capability of these universities. This would also require further training to improve the English proficiency of academic staff, which would facilitate:<br>• access to academic resources in English to inform Turkish-medium teaching and research<br>• promotion in the URAP rankings for these universities. |

## 6.3 Impact analysis: languages of instruction

The languages used for instruction in Turkish universities vary and often undermine academic needs and efficiency. The entry level of most students is too low to benefit fully from EMI tuition, even after a year of preparatory school. Students' mostly want English for longer-term occupational reasons rather than academic needs. In this report three recommendations are made regarding the languages used for instruction. This section summarises what could be achieved if these recommendations of this report are implemented in full:

| Step | Action | Recommendation | Impact |
|---|---|---|---|
| 1 | Turkish-medium instruction | *It is recommended that more focus, status and resources should be given to TMI programmes.* | Turkish-medium programmes would become more attractive to students and parents. Students would learn their specialist subjects more efficiently in their mother tongue, improving academic quality. |

| Step | Action | Recommendation | Impact |
|---|---|---|---|
| | | *It is suggested that TMI programmes should be introduced parallel to existing EMI programmes, and that students should be permitted to access programmes in either or both languages, and should able to choose which language they are assessed in.* | Students wanting an element of EMI would be able to access lectures in English.<br>International students could access EMI programmes.<br>Academic staff would gain practice in teaching in English. |
| 2 | **English-medium instruction** | *While it is not recommended that current undergraduate EMI programmes should be phased out, it is suggested that new ones should not be introduced until secondary schools produce graduates with intermediate CEFR B1) levels of English proficiency.* | The academic quality of programmes would not be threatened by students' inadequate levels of English proficiency. |
| | | *It is also recommended that the focus of new EMI programmes should be at the graduate rather than the undergraduate level.* | More graduate EMI programmes would attract more international students and staff. |
| 3 | **Mixed-medium instruction** | *No new mixed-medium T-EMI programmes should be authorised* | Students could concentrate on their academic subjects without having their progress impeded by trying to comprehend content delivered |

| Step | Action | Recommendation | Impact |
|---|---|---|---|
| | | and existing T-EMI programmes should be phased out as soon as possible, given contextual constraints, and replaced by parallel EMI and TMI programmes. | in English. Academic quality and motivation would be improved. |

## 6.4 Impact analysis: English language teaching and learning in universities

In this report, the current situation in Turkish universities has been surveyed at a number of levels – international, national, institutional and departmental. It is evident that the root cause of Turkey's 'English deficit' is the problems in the school system and these will take a generation to rectify. In the meantime, universities have little choice but to operate with an intake whose English level is 'rudimentary' – even after 1,000+ hours (estimated at end of Grade 12) of English classes'[135]. Under these circumstances (as was stated in Section 3.1.1) it is 'virtually impossible'[136] to reach the target level of B2 in the eight months of the preparatory school programme – they are expected to do too much with too many students in too little time. The central problem is students' motivation, and all the measures set out here are aimed at improving motivation.

In this section a summary is given of what could be achieved if certain recommendations of this report are implemented in full in a series of eleven steps:

| Step | Action | Recommendation | Impact |
|---|---|---|---|
| 1 | Reduced eligibility | Preparatory classes should normally be available only to EMI students. | Reduced intake and improved motivation as English classes are seen as broadly relevant to the medium of instruction. |
| 2 | Raised entry standard | The threshold for entry for EMI students should be raised to CEFR A2. | Improved intake, although it must be stated that (by European standards) CEFR A2 is still very low. |
| 3 | Improved entry assessment | The entry level should be assessed through valid university entrance | The university entrance examinations will provide a motivating target for candidates. |

---
[135] Vale *et al* 2013:16
[136] Vale *et al* 2013:16

| Step | Action | Recommendation | Impact |
|---|---|---|---|
|  |  | examinations assessing all four skills. |  |
| 4 | **Revised curriculum** | *The curriculum should be shifted away from English for General Purposes (EGP) towards English for General Academic Purposes (EGAP), and EGAP classes should be customised to cater for students' specialist academic fields.* | Motivation will be improved because students would not be repeating what they failed to learn several times in school, and because they will now see the relevance of the curriculum to their academic studies. |
| 5 | **In-service teacher development** | *All English teachers should undergo a short, intensive training programme in ESP/EAP, and some teachers in each university should be offered longer-term training such as that available by distance from some universities.* | English teachers will have the confidence and the skills to teach a more relevant curriculum, using materials which they could adapt and customise to students' academic disciplines. Students' extrinsic motivation would be improved by a curriculum and materials which are perceived as relevant. |
| 6 | **Communicative methodology** | *All teachers should undergo training in techniques for incorporating student-student interaction at every stage of the lesson, with speaking integrated into every activity, regardless of the skill being practised.* | Teachers would have the skills and confidence to deliver more interactive lessons. Students' speaking skills and confidence would be improved. Students' intrinsic motivation would be improved by more dynamic lessons. |

| Step | Action | Recommendation | Impact |
|---|---|---|---|
| 7 | Revised exit standards | The exit standards for preparatory school should be revised: CEFR B2 in all skills for linguistically-demanding programmes[137]; CEFR B1+ in all skills for linguistically less-demanding programmes[138]. | If stages 1-6 are implemented, these exit standards are a) achievable and b) minimally adequate for EMI study. They would provide realistic and motivating standards for students. |
| 8 | Improved exit assessment | The exit level should be assessed through valid preparatory school exit examinations assessing all four skills. | A rigorous and valid exit examination would provide a realistic and motivating standard for students and a positive 'washback effect'. |
| 9 | Redirection | Students who do not meet these exit standards should be redirected to TMI programmes or universities. | Another stage providing extrinsic motivation. Note: It is also recommended that the status and resources of TMI programmes should be improved so that they should not be seen as 'second best' (6.1.2). |
| 10 | Revised distribution of English teaching programmes | Credit-bearing English language courses should be maintained throughout all undergraduate and graduate programmes. These courses should be requirements for all EMI students but elective for TMI students. | Students would receive the English language support they need throughout all the years of their studies. |
| 11 | Work-related English | An elective English for Occupational Purposes (EOP) | All students would have an opportunity to acquire work-related English at a time when they will be |

[137] e.g. Engineering, Pure Sciences, Medicine, Law, Journalism, Business, etc.
[138] e.g. Technology, Pure Mathematics, Agriculture, etc.

| Step | Action | Recommendation | Impact |
|---|---|---|---|
| | | course should be available in the final undergraduate year for those seeking jobs. | most motivated to learn it. |

## 6.5 Impact analysis: English as medium of instruction

Although the English proficiency of most academics teaching through English is adequate, two major problems have been identified:

- Senior academics in many institutions reported that there is a shortage of academics with the necessary levels of English proficiency to teach their specialist subjects.

- The teaching styles of most EMI academics fail to accommodate the language problems of their students.

| Step | Action | Recommendation | Impact |
|---|---|---|---|
| 1 | **Improved EMI teaching** | *The approach to English-mediated education should be shifted from traditional English Medium Instruction (EMI), where the lecturer takes little or no responsibility for the language used, to Content and Language Integrated Learning (CLIL), in which the lecturer uses strategies which take account of students' language limitations, in line with developments in most European countries.* | Academic lecturers would feel more confident and effective when teaching through the medium of English.<br><br>Students would receive the English language support they need throughout all the years of their studies. |
| 2 | **Training for EMI lecturers** | *EMI academics should be required to undergo training* | Students' learning load would be reduced as lecturers 'accommodate' their language |

| Step | Action | Recommendation | Impact |
|---|---|---|---|
| 2 | | *and to take moreresponsibility for their students' learning by adopting a range of language and technological strategies to facilitate learning.* | limitations and employ strategies to ensure that communication and motivation are improved in the academic classroom. |

## 6.6 Conclusions

This baseline study is the result of large-scale, widespread research into a cross-section of universities across the whole of Turkey. The findings and recommendations are all based on this research, and evidence has been provided at every stage, and areas indicated where further research is needed before major policy decisions could be made. The picture that emerges is that of a healthy and expanding university system, but one which will need to continue to grow and improve if it is to keep pace with the country's needs and contribute to its economic and social development. Problems have been identified – systemic as well as pedagogic. The most positive finding is that wherever a shortcoming has been identified, there is nearly always a ready-made solution at one or more universities elsewhere in the system which has addressed the issue and devised and implemented a solution. For this reason, it can be stated with confidence that the recommendations contained in this report are feasible and practical, and, in most cases, already in operation at one or more institutions. Turkish universities are particularly willing to share their experience and good examples of regional co-operation were found in various parts of the country, as well as the beginnings of several nationwide initiatives.

The British Council always stands ready to work with various partners in the higher education sector to develop the recommendations and solutions suggested in this baseline study.

# References

Adams J, C King, D Pendlebury, D Hook & J Wilsdon — 2011 — *Global Research Report: Middle East, Leeds*: Thomson Reuters

Aykel A & Y Özek — 2010 — 'A language needs analysis research at an English medium university in Turkey', *Procedia - Social and Behavioral Sciences*, 2 pages 969-75

BALEAP — 2008 — *Competency Framework for Teachers of English for Academic Purposes* (available online at www.baleap.org.uk)

Barnett P & C Lascar — 2012 — *Comparing unique title coverage of Web of Science and Scopus in Earth and Atmospheric Sciences'* [http://www.istl.org/12-summer.refereed3.html]

Başaran S & F Hayta — 2013 — 'A correlational study of Turkish students' motivation to learn English', *Electronic Journal of Education Sciences* 2/3, pages 104-115

Başıbek N. M Dolmacı, B Ceyda Cengiz, B Bür, Y Dilek & B Kara — 2013 — 'Lecturers' perceptions of English medium instruction at engineering departments of higher education: a study on partial English medium instruction at some state universities in Turkey', *Procedia – Social and Behavioral Sciences* 111, pages 1819-25

Bektaş-Çetinkaya Y — 2012 — 'Turkish university students' motivation to learn English: integration into international community', *Hacettepe Üniversitesi Eğitim Fakültesi Dergisi* 43, pages 130-140

Berg R van den & A Ross — 1999 — 'The importance of the subjective reality of teachers during the educational innovation: a concerns-based approach', *American Educational Research Journal,* 36 pages 879-906

Brazeau G — 2006 — 'Handouts in the classroom: is note-taking a lost skill?' *American Pharmaceutical Education* 70/2, article 38, pages 1-2

Çetinsaya G — 2014 — *Büyüme, Kalite, Uluslararasılaşma: Türkiye Yükseköğretimi İçin Bir Yol Haritası,*

| | | Ankara: YÖK |
|---|---|---|
| Çokgezen M (2014) | 2014 | 'Determinants of university choice: a study on economics departments in Turkey', *Yükseköğretim Dergisi*, 4/1 |
| Coleman J | 2006 | 'English-medium teaching in European higher education', *Language Teaching* 39/1, pages 1-14 |
| Collins A | 2010 | 'English-medium higher education: dilemmas and problems', *Eğitim Araştırmaları-Eurasian Journal of Educational Research* 39 pages 91-110 |
| Darn S | n/d | *Content and Language Integrated Learning (CLIL): A European Overview* (Available online at www.researchgate.net/publication/234652746) |
| Day J & M Krzanowski | 2011 | *Teaching English for Specific Purposes: An Introduction. Cambridge:* Cambridge University Press. (Available online at: http://peo.cambridge.org/images/espbooklet.pdf) |
| Dearden J | 2014 | *English as a Medium of Instruction – a Growing Global Phenomenon*, London: British Council (Available online at http://www.britishcouncil.org/sites/britishcouncil.uk2/files/e484_emi_-_cover_option_3_final_web.pdf) |
| Doğancay-Aktuna S & Z Kızıltepe | 2005 | 'English in Turkey', *World Englishes* 24/2 pages 253-65 |
| Education First | 2014 | *EF EPI-c – EF English Proficiency Index for Companies* [available online at www.ef.com/epic] |
| Füruzan V | 2012 | 'Adaptation to the Bologna Process: The Case of Turkey', *Excellence in Higher Education*, 2, pages 101-10 |
| Graddol D | 2006 | *English Next*, London: British Council |
| Harbord J | 1992 | 'The use of the mother tongue in the |

| | | |
|---|---|---|
| | | classroom', *English Language Teaching Journal* 46/4 pages 350-55 |
| Jordan R | 1998 | *English for Academic Purposes*, Cambridge: Cambridge University Press |
| Jordan R | 2002 | `The growth of EAP in Britain,' *Journal of English for Academic Purposes* 1/1, pages 69-78 |
| Kılıçkaya F | 2006 | 'Instructors' Attitudes towards English-Medium Instruction in Turkey', *Humanising Language Teaching* 8/6 pages 1-16 |
| Kırkgöz Y | 2005 | 'Motivation and student perception of studying in an English-medium university', *Journal of Language and Linguistic Studies* 1/1 pages 101-23 |
| Kırkgöz Y | 2009 | 'Students' and lecturers' perceptions of the effectiveness of foreign language instruction in an English-medium university in Turkey', *Teaching in Higher Education* 14/1 pages 81-93 |
| Kırkgöz Y | 2014 | 'Students' perceptions of English language versus Turkish language used as the medium of instruction in higher education in Turkey', *Turkish Studies* 9/12 pages 443-59 |
| Klaassen R & E de Graaff | 2001 | 'Facing innovation: preparing lecturers for English-medium instruction in a non-native context', *European Journal of Engineering Education*, 26/3 pages 281-89 |
| Koru S & J Åkesson | 2011 | *Turkey's English Deficit*, Ankara: TEPAV |
| Maurenen A, N Hynninen & E Ranta | 2010 | 'English as an academic lingua franca: The ELFA project', *English for Specific Purposes* 29/3 pages 183-90 |
| Murdoch G | 2000 | 'Introducing a teacher supportive evaluation system', *English Language Teaching Journal* 54/1 pages 54-64 |
| Özoğlu M, B S Gür & İ Coşkun | 2012 | Küresel Eğilimler Işığında Türkiye'de Uluslararası Öğrenciler, Ankara: SETA |

| | | |
|---|---|---|
| Özcan Y Z | 2011 | *Challenges to the Turkish Higher Education System*, paper given at the 22nd International Conference on Higher Education, Bilkent University, Ankara, June 17-19, 2011 |
| Ruiz-Garrido M & M Campoy-Cubillo (eds) | 2013 | 'CLIL at university: research and developments', *Language Value* 5/1 |
| Scott M, L Carioni, M Zanetta, E Bayer & T Quintanilha | 1984 | 'Using a "standard exercise" in teaching reading comprehension, *English Language Teaching Journal* 38/2 pages 114-20 |
| Sert N | 2008 | `The language of instruction dilemma in the Turkish context', *System* 36/2 pages 156-71 |
| Shatrova Z | 2014 | `Teaching English to Engineering Students in the ContemporaryWorld: A Case Study on Ukrainian and Turkish Universities', *Journal of Education and Practice* 11/5, pages 149-56 |
| Shepherd E | 2013 | *The Importance of International Education: a perspective from Turkish students,* Hong Kong: British Council |
| Swales J | 1984 | 'Thoughts on, in and outside the ESP classroom', in James G (ed) *The ESP Classroom – Methodology, Materials, Expectations,* Exeter: University of Exeter Press, pages 7-16 |
| Thompson I | 1987 | 'Turkish speakers' in Swan M & B Smith (eds), *Learner English*, Cambridge: Cambridge University Press, pages 158-69 |
| Toköz Göktepe F | 2014 | 'Attitudes and motivation of Turkish undergraduate EFL students towards learning English language, *Studies in English Language Teaching* 2/3 |
| Tung P, R Lam & W Tsang | 1997 | 'English as a medium of instruction in post-1997 Hong Kong: What students, teachers and parents think', *Journal of Pragmatics* 28, pages 441-59 |
| Vale D, E Özen, | 2013 | *Turkey National Needs Assessment of State* |

| | | |
|---|---|---|
| I Alpaslan, A Çağlı, I Özdoğan, M Sancak, A Dizman & A Sökmen | | *School English Language Teaching*, Ankara: British Council and TEPAV |
| Van Weijen D | 2012 | 'The language of (future) scientific communication', *Research Trends* 31 [www.researchtrends.com/issue-31-november-2012] |
| West R | 1994 | 'Needs analysis in language teaching', *Language Teaching* 27/1, pages 1-19 |
| West R | 2013 | *MA in ELT English for Specific Purposes Module Materials*, Reading: University of Reading |
| Westerheijden D, E Beerkens, L Cremonini, B Kehm, A Kovac. P Lažetič, A McCoshan, N Mozuraityté, M Souto Otero, E de Weert, J Witte & Y Yağcı | 2010 | *The Bologna Process Independent Assessment: The First Decade of Working on the European Higher Education Area, Volume 2 – Case Studies and Appendices, Chapter 6* Turkey, Kassel: Center for Higher Education Policy Studies, pages 93-103 |
| Yağcı Y | 2010 | 'A different view of the Bologna Process: the case of Turkey', *European Journal of Education* 45/4 pages 588-600 |
| Yakışık H | 2012 | *Can the Bologna Process Improve Turkish Education System?* (accessed 13/04/2015) |
| YÖK | 2014 | *Higher Education System in Turkey*, Ankara: YÖK |